The L... said ... not ... b... ... make ... a help.

Genesis Chap. 2. Ver. 18.

The
*Eternal Woman*
Library

# HISTORY OF BENEDICTINE NUNS

# HISTORY
# OF
# BENEDICTINE NUNS

*by*

STEPHANUS HILPISCH, O.S.B.

*Translated by*

SISTER M. JOANNE MUGGLI, O.S.B.

*Edited by*

LEONARD J. DOYLE

## ST. JOHN'S ABBEY PRESS

COLLEGEVILLE                *1958*                MINNESOTA

The original work, *Geschichte der Benediktinerinnen,* is Volume III of the collection *Benediktinisches Geistesleben,* edited by Dr. Heinrich Suso Brechter, O.S.B. It was published in 1951 by the Archabbey of St. Ottilien.

*Nihil obstat:* Gregory J. Roettger, O.S.B. *Censor deputatus*

*Imprimatur:* ✠Peter W. Bartholome, D.D., Bishop of St. Cloud. May 28, 1957.

The *Nihil obstat* and the *Imprimatur* are ecclesiastical declarations that a publication is free of doctrinal or moral error, not a statement of the positive worth, nor an implication that the contents have the Bishop's approval or recommendation.

# Foreword

The history of Benedictine monachism is presented in another volume under the title *Benedictinism through Changing Centuries*. The present *History of Benedictine Nuns* is a supplement. Since the great monastic movements of Cluny, Hirsau, Bursfeld and others were described in detail in the former work, this information is not repeated in the present volume. I believe that I am rendering a service to the convents of our order with this book, since there is hardly a single publication on the history of Benedictine nuns available.

I have taken particular pains to work out the lines of development and to present the recurring influence of the monasteries on the convents. The Benedictine nuns did not make Benedictine history. This is not woman's work. But in every era in which the ideal of the monastic life was recognized and proclaimed pure and undefiled by the monks, the nuns lived it in still greater purity and devotion. Often when the holy flame was already extinct in the monasteries, the nuns still guarded the light of Christ in their convents. This is the great contribution they have made to Benedictine history.

The present work is also an expression of my gratitude for all the kindness I have been shown in the three convents which bear the spiritual and monastic stamp of the abbey of Maria Laach—convents in which I could often sojourn and in whose life I was permitted to participate in some way: St. Hildegard in Eibingen, Holy Cross in Herstelle and St. Mary at Fulda. Special thanks are due the venerable sisters who guard the heritage of St. Lioba at the grave of St. Boniface in Fulda. In their convent I found the leisure to write this book, stimulated by the pure air of this garden of God and protected by its silence. Hearing their psalmody, giving their spiritual conferences, contemplating their artistic works and receiving their sisterly hospitality, invisible and yet effective, I relived the past.

I have written this booklet also in tribute to our young women who love Christ and follow Him, and who even today long for the totality and the fulness of the Christ-life. They have shown themselves particularly responsive to the prompting of the Spirit of God, who in our times has reawakened in the Church a love for the mysteries of Christ, the Eucharistic sacrifice and the psalmody. In St. Benedict's sanctuary an opportunity is given them to participate in the sacred Mysteries in a manner scarcely to be found elsewhere in this world.

The time-honored abbey of Nonnberg at Salzburg, the oldest German-speaking convent, should be mentioned also; for the very valuable information which was given to me there, I express my humble thanks.

This fruit of my labors I offer to my esteemed co-religious in the convents of St. Benedict and to our young people. In keeping with the purpose of this book, I have done away with footnotes and merely indicated a few sources.

Stephanus Hilpisch, O.S.B.

Fulda, July 20, 1950.

# Contents

# Contents

# HISTORY OF BENEDICTINE NUNS

# CHAPTER 1

# BEGINNINGS OF WOMEN'S COMMUNITIES

When monachism was just making its appearance in the Church—about the year 300—and starting the rapid development which would soon bring it to a position of great influence not only in the ascetic but also in the intellectual and cultural domain, the institute of VIRGINS CONSECRATED TO GOD could already look back over a long period of existence.[1] It was of apostolic origin and had received the approval of St. Paul himself. In Corinth, young women chose the single life for Christ the Lord, to serve only the One wholeheartedly.

Known as "God's chosen ones," as "holy virgins," as "brides of Christ" and by other glorious titles, these virgins were highly esteemed by the faithful. They were considered as espoused to the Lord; and just as a wife receives dignity and honor through her husband, so did these virgins through Christ the Lord. According to Tertullian, the dowry presented to their Bridegroom was their prayers offered to God day and night—an evidence that from the very beginning the psalmody was theirs as a special function. The high esteem which they enjoyed is shown by the fact that they occupied a place of honor at the divine services and that they were commemorated in public prayer as a distinct state of life.

After the beginning of the third century the veil became their distinguishing mark, which they, like married women, wore. As the married woman appeared in public with the veil and was thereby protected against any advances, so the consecrated virgin

---

[1]Iniga Feussi, *Das Institut der gottgeweihten Jungfrauen*, Fribourg, Switzerland, 1917. Translator's note: See J. A. Campbell, *Virgins Consecrated to God in Rome during the First Centuries*, American Catholic Quarterly Review 25, 1900, 766-790.

was recognized by the veil and considered sacred, the more so as the bishop himself had given her the veil when she made her vow of virginity.

Aside from preserving virginity, whence they received their name, the virgins had no particular religious or ascetical obligations, though bishops and teachers of the spiritual life as early as the third century admonished them to the practices considered protective of chastity: simplicity of dress and manner of life, a certain degree of poverty, charitable works, reading, a secluded life and fasting. Originally they made their vows privately, but in the third century they began to pronounce them before the bishop and the community, and it was not long before the profession of vows was accompanied by a consecration.

The virgins soon found within the community an activity suitable to their state: caring for the poor and assisting with the instruction and baptism of women catechumens. By reason of this activity they functioned under the direction of the bishops in a special manner as a sort of "female clergy." Like the clerics they lived with their families, but we do hear of an early attempt at community life. Some virgins chose an ascetic as guardian and teacher; in return, they cared for him and lived in his house. This mode of life, however, the so-called SUBINTRODUCTION, caused scandal in the community, and because of its inherent dangers was opposed and forbidden by the bishops. On the other hand, the virgins sometimes banded together into communities in the larger cities. Such a community, called a parthenon[2] or house of virgins, was entrusted by St. Anthony to his younger sister when he withdrew into solitude about the year 280.

With the rise of monasticism and the resulting intensification and propagation of the ascetic ideal, the desire for the consecrated life received a new impulse among women. We can now identify two great movements. The *monachae* attached themselves closely to the monks so as to lead the life of the spirit in a more complete withdrawal from the world, in mortification and in ascetic practices. The other group, in conformity with their tradition, remained in the world and gave further formation to the state of *virgines sacrae* under the direction of the bishops. Instead

[2]Translator's note: See E. C. Butler, *Cambridge Medieval History* I, Cambridge, England, 1936, 521. See also Philibert Schmitz, O.S.B., *Histoire de l'Ordre de S. Benoît* VII, Maredsous, Belgium, 1956, 17, footnote (4).

of following a rule, the virgins lived according to the canons set up by the bishops. Beyond that, they had complete freedom, especially significant with regard to the disposal of their property. If the virgins were "women clerics," the nuns were "women monks."

The old asceticism and the state of virginity had already considered such things as withdrawal from the world and complete dedication to Christ as an ideal, and had lived them in some manner. Under monachism these ideals received definite form, a certain enhancement and, through exterior conventionalities, a protection against the dangers threatening ascetics and virgins living in the world, dangers to which many were succumbing. The exterior practices were complete renunciation of property and all earthly things, unconditional obedience toward authority, community life, uniformity in dress, and a life of prayer and work according to a narrowly prescribed norm.

High as were the praises of the life of virginity in the third century, the complaints were correspondingly sharp. Criticism was directed at the great wealth of individual virgins, their avarice and hardheartedness, their pride, their vanity, their unseemly deportment in public, their disobedience to the requests of the bishops, and also their violations of chastity.

Monasticism, or the acceptance of women under monasticism, put an end to these abuses. Here the virgin gave up all the wealth she possessed and separated herself from her family, from parish life and from public activity. She lived a life of renunciation, prayer and work according to the rule and instructions of a spiritual master. It is not surprising that this monastic form of life attracted numerous ascetically inclined virgins.

As the old asceticism certainly still existed along with monachism, so the state of virginity in the world maintained its position, to disappear only in the ninth century and then to acquire new life in the institution of canonesses. But the future belonged to the nuns, the ascetic women of the new era. Their institution was supported by the strong ascetic movement that had seized the imagination of Christendom in the fourth and fifth centuries and had found its patrons and promoters in the great Church Fathers: Athanasius, Basil, Gregory Nazianzen, Ambrose, Jerome and Augustine.

Just as we know that St. Pachomius († 436) was the founder of monasticism proper and the first monk to live in a monastery, so we also know that Mary, sister of Pachomius, was the first nun. She joined her brother, and he built a convent for her and her companions near his monastery at Tabennisi about the year 330. In a short time there were almost 400 nuns here, and a second convent according to the Rule of Pachomius[3] was established.

The convents as well as the monasteries were under the general direction of Pachomius and his successors; but, like the monasteries, every convent had its own government. The nuns were obliged to be obedient to the mother, who ruled the entire household and had charge of all. The mode of life was similar to that of the monks. The nuns kept the two great prayer hours, evening and early morning, and throughout the day all worked in individual houses. All were urged to learn reading and writing, and to memorize a part of holy Scripture, especially the Psalms. They observed fasting on certain days and silence every day. In quick succession convents sprang up in Egypt, Syria, Palestine and Asia Minor following the pattern of Tabennisi.

Influenced by St. Jerome, the noble Roman matron Paula († 404) with her daughter Eustochium founded three convents at Bethlehem near the grotto of our Lord's nativity about the year 389. St. Jerome translated the Rule of Pachomius for these convents "to give Eustochium something she could transmit to her sisters." The nuns at Bethlehem lived largely according to the statutes of Pachomius, but they soon added special house rules, as St. Jerome has also informed us.[4] Each of the three convents had its own mother, but the management of the entire community was in Paula's hands.

There was a common oratory in which the nuns assembled for the psalmody. On Sundays all attended the celebration of the Eucharist in the church of the Manger of our Lord. At night they arose for the Vigils and furthermore kept the canonical Hours of the early morning, Terce, Sext and None during the day, and Vespers in the evening. As soon as the hour for prayer approached in each convent, a nun called out "Alleluia" in a loud voice, and thereupon all hastened to the oratory. The whole psalter was sung every day and had to be memorized. At the prayer hours individual nuns, each in her turn, recited one or more psalms while

---

[3]Ed. by P. B. Albers, Florilegium Patr. 16, Bonn 1925; ed. by A. Boon and L. Th. Lefort, *Pachomiana Latina*, Louvain 1932.
[4]Letter 108, Migne 22, 896 ff.

the others listened in silence; this was the way in which the Egyptian convents also held their prayer hours. There was daily reading of Scripture, which Jerome explained in conferences for the community of nuns. The time not spent in prayer and reading was devoted to work, such as sewing their own clothing. The nuns wore a simple woolen garment, and no one held any personal property.

Because of the esteem in which St. Jerome, St. Paula and St. Eustochium were held, the convents at Bethlehem became renowned: many young women entered here; both men and women came as pilgrims; and several women, after returning to their homeland, founded convents after the model of Bethlehem.

Not long after the building of the convent at the grotto of our Lord's nativity, St. MELANIA the Elder († 410) founded a convent on the Mount of Olives in Jerusalem. Through her influence and that of her granddaughter Melania the Younger († 439), this convent was to attain a renown like that of St. Paula's foundation. About the same time, St. BASIL († 379) founded a convent which his mother Emmelia and his sister Macrina entered. Like Pachomius, Basil based the constitution for his convent closely on the norms which he had laid down for his monks. In both places it was customary that the monks take over the spiritual direction of the nuns.

Toward the end of the fourth century, the first convents for nuns were founded in the great cities of the West, Rome and Milan, followed by others in Florence, Bologna, Pisa, Vercelli and other cities. The two great doctors of the Church, Ambrose and Augustine, bestowed their loving pastoral care on these young foundations and brought large numbers of young women to the convents through their enthusiastic sermons.

The name of St. AUGUSTINE in particular is permanently associated with religious institutions for women. What St. Pachomius had been for the East, St. Augustine became for the West. Because of strife within a convent in which his own sister ruled and in which the nuns desired a new superior, the saint addressed a letter to the community urging peace and unity.[5] He used this opportunity to give the nuns a number of admonitions and precepts on which to pattern their mode of life. It is not evident

[5]Letter 211, Migne 33, 958ff. Translator's note: See Gerald Ellard, S. J., *Saintly Sisters in the Shadows*, Review for Religious 4, 1945, 155-162.

from this one letter whether he wished to remind them of precepts already existing or whether he was giving them new ones.

His moral teaching emphasizes especially unity, love, humility and obedience. There may be no private ownership in the convent. The Office is to be recited at the hours appointed by the Church and in the customary manner. A uniform garb does not seem to be customary as yet, for in this regard he says merely, "Your clothing should not be showy, and you should strive to please not by your dress but by your conduct." The hair is not cut, but covered with a net, over which a veil is placed so that the hair cannot be seen. The regulation that a bath be permitted every month is generous; to the sick it is permitted even more frequently. Claustral enclosure is unknown to the saint; but at an appearance in public, great reserve is commanded. At the head of the house is the mother, with a priest to assist her "who takes care of all of you" and whom she is to notify of everything "which is beyond her nature or strength."

This letter, the so-called Rule of St. Augustine, had far-reaching effects and greatly influenced the development of monasticism for both monks and nuns. Written for very definite conditions and emanating from a particular situation, it became a general statute, which even today has not lost its influence. This is due not only to the authority of the writer but also to the contents of the letter. In contrast to the Rule of Pachomius, Augustine's Rule keeps the concrete subservient to basic principles.

With characteristic openness of heart and greatness of soul, and with the proficiency in the care of souls which is no less characteristic of him, the saint has depicted the ideal of monastic community life in a few monumental strokes and in such a way that it can be carried out by women. After barely 100 years of monasticism there already appeared the great danger of placing too much emphasis on the ascetic practices of monks, giving them undue significance. So Augustine called for the original aim to which monasticism owed its formation, Christlikeness, practiced in the virtues of love and humility. Few details are ordered, and these are well weighed, balanced and moderated. All regulations are presented as maxims concisely stated, and the particulars of monastic life are conceived and arranged with the essence of that life in view. These features made a rule out of the letter, a rule from which St. Benedict also profited.

At the beginning of the fifth century, the esteemed father of monks, CASSIAN († about 435), to whom we are indebted for exact knowledge of the old monasticism and who left a widely read work on asceticism in his *Conferences of the Fathers,* was the director of a convent in Marseille. Gaul was soon to become a land of convents. Already before the year 400 the first convents were founded in Spain, and during the fifth century the first ones were founded in Ireland. The Irish as well as the Spanish followed the early traditions of the East, but their own national influences still made themselves felt.

A Spanish nun, Aetheria, undertook a pilgrimage to the Holy Land toward the end of the fourth century. She left an accurate account of this journey, describing the divine services held in the holy places, a report classed as one of the most important documents of liturgical history. Her travelogue shows clearly the high spiritual ideals a nun of that epoch had, and also shows that she was truly a sister to the monks, in whom culture was taken for granted.

As with many human institutions, so with the institution of religious life for women, the first century, from about 350 to 450, was a golden era. The new dignity of woman, which Christianity had effected, showed its impressive results for the first time after the barriers to the development of community life had been lifted by the acceptance of Christianity as the state religion. During the period of persecution, consecrated virginity could not be widely recognized except in certain areas. Only in northern Africa,[6] where because of especially favorable circumstances Christianity held a unique position and was strong enough to live in the open, did consecrated virginity figure more prominently in the life of the community.

The vocation to consecrated virginity and to the cloister opened entirely new possibilities to the Christian woman. Under

[6]Translator's note: Butler in *Cambridge Medieval History* I, 30-31 says, "The famous Coptic Abbot Senuti of Atripe governed a great community of nuns in addition to the monks of the White Monastery. We learn from Palladius that at the end of the fourth century there were numerous nunneries in all parts of monastic Egypt, and the glimpses he lets us see of their inner life are graphic and interesting. He tells of one Dorotheus who had the spiritual charge of a nunnery and used to sit at a window overlooking the convent, 'keeping the peace among the nuns'; also, of an old nun, Mother Talis, superioress of a convent at Attinoe, so beloved by her nuns that there was no need of a key in that convent, as in others, to keep the nuns from wandering, 'as they were fast tied by love of her.' "

the influence of the religious fervor of the fourth century, thoroughly ascetic in character, enthusiasm for the ideal of consecrated virginity resulted in a powerful Christian women's movement, which attracted the noblest souls of the times. These women were concerned, not with their rights or the removal of limitations, but with the fulfillment of womanhood through intellectual and spiritual values.

It was significant and decisive for the future that the great Church leaders and teachers recognized that hour as the hour of the Christian woman. In their sermons as well as in their writings, they became the inspired heralds of the new ideal for women. Many, like Jerome and even Ambrose, went to such lengths in their praises of the life of virginity that they could be suspected of failing to appreciate matrimony. How effective the oratory was, is shown by the fact that the aristocratic women in Milan no longer permitted their daughters to attend the sermons of Ambrose for fear that they would take the nun's veil and reject the suitor already chosen for them.

To remain unmarried was no longer a misfortune, much less a disgrace; on the contrary, virginity ranked high in meaning and purpose. Here was a new evaluation of the personality of woman. She did not require a husband to be esteemed and through him to find the fulness of life within the family. Indeed, the virgin could even attain a higher dignity than the married woman. As the latter received her dignity through the wealth and position of her husband, so the virgin received hers through religious consecration and through Christ the Lord, to whom she was espoused.

In the ascetic life woman received the opportunity for suitable self-development and a corresponding mission, work in a convent, with a community of sisters banded together for the same lofty purpose. Within this community, thanks to her womanhood, she could work out the virtues of humility, love and chastity much more readily and purely than it is given to men to do.

Important also in the development of convents was the fact that a large proportion of the women who entered them came from the higher classes, and these quite naturally gave the convents a certain refinement. Nowhere did the nuns, any more than the monks, exclude people of the lower classes. To do so would have been quite un-Christian. It stands to reason, however, that superiors like Paula, Eustochium, Melania, Marcella and Macrina influenced the formation of their nuns and virgins in a very definite way. This explains why the convents turned to intellectual pursuits from the very beginning. The nuns were just as much interested in books as the monks were.

How could the intellectual life be neglected when Ambrose, Jerome, Augustine and Rufinus were the spiritual fathers of the nuns! It was the women who listened to them most eagerly. Many ascetical and theological problems which challenged the teachers of the fourth century were first discussed with the nuns. Jerome had made it clear that the true nun is a student; his letter on the education of Laeta was the foundation for the later development of the intellectual life in convents.

Until the beginning of the sixth century the nuns, apart from those convents in which the letter of St. Augustine was the norm of life, almost without exception followed rules originally written for monks. This was due to their close association with the monks and the spiritual care received from them. At that time the holy Bishop CAESARIUS of Arles (†542), like many bishops a friend and promoter of monasteries and convents—he himself had been a monk at Lérins—undertook to write a rule[7] of his own for the nuns of the convent at Arles, in which his sister Caesaria was superior. He realized that a convent differed from a monastery in many respects, and so he wished to write a rule which would be suitable especially for women.

The rule itself kept close to St. Augustine's letter in many points, but added such minute details that it is possible to form an accurate picture of the nun's life in a convent of the sixth century. The whole exposition shows great esteem for nuns and breathes the spirit of gentleness and love. Epoch-making was the precept of the *clausura* as a complete separation from the world and enclosure within the convent walls. The convent was within the city. How could the life of the nuns within a large city be protected unless a complete separation from the world were effected? There was no communication with the outside world, and the nuns were not even permitted to enter the nave of the basilica. Besides the abbess there was a *provisor* to take care of exterior needs. Priests and clergymen who came to the convent to cele-

[7]Ed. by G. Morin, Florilegium Patr. 34, Bonn 1933. Translator's note: See Eleanor Shipley Duckett, *The Gateway to the Middle Ages*, New York 1938, 396, 411-416.

brate Mass were obliged to leave immediately after the service. The nuns recited the Divine Office according to the manner of the monastery at Lérins.

The time not devoted to prayer was spent in reading and handwork. All had to learn to write, as they were to occupy themselves in copying manuscripts. When they were engaged in handwork, someone read aloud whenever possible. Children of seven years of age could be accepted into the convent to be educated, but only those destined for convent life. The garb of the nuns was white; black, which at that time was a sign of nobility, as well as brightly colored clothing, was forbidden. The hair was concealed by a veil. In chapter 56 of his rule Caesarius gives the maximum height of the coiffure: the hair should not be worn high according to the fashion of that time. All private ownership was forbidden, of course. Beyond that, the greatest simplicity was demanded by the rejection of every luxury, and even in the church nothing costly should be found, not even any colorful pictures.

The Rule of Caesarius spread in Gaul, although it did not become the only norm for convents. Bishop AURELIAN of Arles († 549), the second successor of Caesarius, gave a new foundation in Arles its own rule, but based it on that of Caesarius.

The most important convent following the Rule of Caesarius was Holy Cross in POITIERS, in which Queen Radigund lived and which her foster-daughter Agnes ruled as abbess. Here the poet Venantius Fortunatus, chaplain from 542 to 562, composed the hymn *Vexilla regis prodeunt* for the translation of a relic of the Cross to the convent.

Through the protection of the bishops and the nobility the convents received a new impetus. Convents as well as monasteries, because of their great landed property and the education of their members, took an important place in ecclesiastical and cultural life. Many noblewomen, even princesses and queens, became nuns. Among them were the daughters of King Guntram († 592), Clodeburg and Clothilde.

That the reception of princesses could be detrimental is shown by an episode in the convent of Poitiers, which led to an insurrection. Crodechild,[8] daughter of King Charibert († 567), and Basina, daughter of King Chilperic († 584), rebelled against their

---

[8]Translator's note: Spelled Chrodield by Lina Eckenstein, *Woman under Monasticism*, 66, and Eleanor Shipley Duckett, *The Gateway to the Middle Ages*, 251.

abbess Teudovera,[9] saying that in the convent they were treated as servants and not as princesses. About 40 nuns joined them. The agitators received support from friends in the city and with their help wanted to expel the abbess from the convent. When the metropolitan of Bordeaux with several bishops came to the convent to establish peace, adherents of the rebellious nuns attacked them, and several of the bishops were ill-treated. Crodechild actually succeeded in taking possession of the abbey, and it was some time before peace was restored.

The convents in Gaul received great help and stimulation through the arrival of St. Columban († 615) and his companions, who came to France from Ireland and worked for the monastic ideal with the zeal of missionaries. Results were especially noticeable among the women, and one convent after another was erected. Some of these convents had a great many nuns. In the sixth century Arles and Poitiers each numbered 200, the convent of Abbess Salaberga had about 300, as did the convent of St. Eligius († about 660) in Paris. Of course, there were also convents with fewer nuns—Montiérender under its first abbess had 60, and others numbered scarcely 20 members.

A description of the life of the convents under Irish influence is given in the rule of the holy Bishop Donatus of Besançon († 656), which he wrote for a convent in his see founded by his mother Flavia.[10] Previously he had been a monk at Luxeuil and so the Rule of Columban was a standard for him. However, he also used the Rule of St. Caesarius and that of St. Benedict very freely. In this way a rule of life was developed which was characteristic of the time: not patterned entirely on any one special rule, but incorporating what seemed good and suitable in each. Thus Donatus took over the idea of white clothing from Caesarius but not the enclosure: with the permission of the abbess the nuns could leave the convent to attend to business transactions.

The fact that conventual discipline was not rigidly fixed but could be adapted to various circumstances had its advantages, but it left the way open to the whims of the individual. Hence the picture of the convents in France in the sixth and seventh centuries was rather variegated, and no less so the picture in Spain and Italy. Everywhere the old saying of Cassian applied: as many

[9]Translator's note: Spelled Leubover by Lina Eckenstein, *op. cit.* 66.
[10]In Migne 87, 273 ff.

rules as convents. Every bishop formulated a rule which seemed good to him, and these were supplemented by the regulations of the abbesses and special house traditions. A single standard to which all submitted was missing.

The condition of groping and searching as well as the multiplicity of forms and norms was brought to an end by the introduction of the Rule of St. Benedict into the convents. This Rule began to achieve success in the beginning of the seventh century, and by the middle of the eighth century victory was decisive. The Rule of St. Benedict became the uniform standard for all convents of the West and remained so until the twelfth century.

# CHAPTER 2

# FOUNDATION OF CONVENTS ACCORDING TO THE RULE OF ST. BENEDICT

The Rule of St. Benedict was written for monks. We know from history that the father of Western monasticism turned his attention only to monasteries. True, an intimate friendship united him closely with his sister Scholastica. She was not a nun, however, but a consecrated virgin living in the world. We learn also from the biography of the saint by Pope Gregory the Great that the holy patriarch of monks communicated with other consecrated virgins who lived in their own home not far from his monastery. But we are not informed that women joined him and requested his guidance in their convents, as was the case with Pachomius and Basil. Neither is it known whether nuns accepted his Rule for their convents on their own initiative or whether it was given to them as a norm of life by bishops or abbots.

That nuns followed rules written for monks was certainly customary. With only a few changes a rule for monks could be adapted for nuns. If this was possible for the rules of Pachomius, Basil and Columban, it was all the more so for the Rule of St. Benedict with its wise moderation and its consideration for the weakness and special needs of individuals.

Perhaps the Rule of St. Benedict was accepted first in the convents of England, where Benedictine monachism witnessed its first great expansion. It does not seem that the monks erected convents for women immediately, for we are told that the young Christian Anglo-Saxon women who desired the conventual life went to Gaul to enter at Faremoutiers or Chelles. At an early period, however, convents were founded in the British Isles; and certainly as soon as monachism spread for monks, the religious life for women also developed. Through the generosity of the kings and nobles numerous convents were founded and endowed with rich landholdings, so that they, like the monasteries, became small manors in which an abbess ruled over land and people. The convents of the earliest period were Barking, Ely, Wenlock, Repton, Whitby, Coldingham, Wimborne, Wilton, Shaftesbury, Winchester, Ramsey and Amesbury.

As in Gaul, so in England the daughters of the nobility flocked to the convents, and indeed some convents seem to have had members only from noble families. There were many nuns of royal blood, and frequently a princess or a former queen ruled as abbess. King Oswy of Northumberland gave his first daughter, one-year-old Aelflaed, to the convent at Hartlepool in gratitude for his victory over Penda of Mercia in the year 655. Mildred, abbess of Minster on the Isle of Thanet, was descended from the same royal family. Ebba († about 680), sister of King Oswy, ruled the convent of Coldingham; Cuthburga († 700), the convent of Wimborne; Queen Edelthryd († 679) was abbess of Ely, where her sister Sexburga († 699) succeeded her in office; her other sister Withburga († about 750) founded the convent of Deorham. Barking had as abbesses three queens and two princesses. It is not surprising that the convents were held in high esteem and that a woman coming from a royal family would take a high position also in the convent, as abbess.

The convents took part in everything that affected the life of the people and the Church. The abbesses appeared in synods and meetings of the people, and their contributions were not ignored, but in fact were often decisive in disputes. As the old pagan Teutons had respected the speech of wise women, so now the opinion of the royal abbesses was honored.

HILDA of Whitby († 680), of the royal family of Northumbria, must be recognized as the outstanding abbess. She participated in the ecclesiastical meeting of 664 held in her convent and played an important role in the controversy over union with Rome or with the Celts. Her successor Aelflaed attended the council at the River Nith in 705, over which Archbishop Brithwald of Canterbury presided. The acts of the synod of Becanheld in 694 were signed by five abbesses.

A feature peculiar to several of the Anglo-Saxon convents was the proximity of a monastery for monks and the centralized government of both communities, which remained separate communities, under the abbess. Hilda's convent at Whitby was a double monastery of this kind, and she was able to make her monastery for monks a training school for bishops, abbots and teachers. The highly renowned poet Caedmon, among others, belonged to her monastery. As Hilda encouraged learning in her convent, so also was learning encouraged at Barking, where the sister and the wife of King Ine entered. The monk Aldhelm (†709) dedicated his poem on virginity to the nuns of Barking. Another intellectually active convent was Wimborne, where Lioba spent her youth.

The first century of the Anglo-Saxon convents was an exceedingly successful period; the convents were generally wealthy; important personalities ruled almost everywhere; and the nuns who sought admission brought with them great eagerness for the religious and the intellectual life. The convents had the same possibilities for expansion with respect to the inner life and worthwhile exterior activities as the monasteries had.

The monasteries for monks or clerics connected with these convents were eager to assist them. Bishops, abbots and monks were kindly disposed toward the convents for nuns, and the monks gave fraternal help wherever these women were in need of it.

The young Anglo-Saxon women harmoniously united real, genuine womanhood and intellectual culture with their striving for religious perfection. One did not know where noble humanity ended and sanctity, the work of grace, began, so organically were the natural and the supernatural bound together. Natural candor, a happy disposition and cheerful behavior were the characteristics of such womanhood. They might lead a nun to write as Egburga did to Boniface, "the true abbot and true friend," that she longed to embrace him with sisterly arms. In all the convents the family spirit was greatly stressed as well as the need for spiritual intercourse and further mental development.

All the nuns enjoyed writing letters and even more receiving them, especially if they came from Germany and brought news of missionary work. Such a letter produced joy in the entire convent and stimulated the nuns to keep praying and working for their missionaries afar. Most letters contained news of the relatives—death or separation from loved ones caused sorrow. The nuns liked to have a spiritual brother or father to whom they opened their hearts and to whom they looked for direction and help in the spiritual life, and to whose approval they could also submit their first shy attempts at the art of writing or even versification.

Keenly interested in the work of the monks in Germany, they copied books and prepared parchments for them. The time was not far distant when they would follow the monks into the foreign lands to assist with the active work of spreading the kingdom of Christ.

The nuns had a great desire for culture, they spoke and wrote Latin fluently, and they accomplished astonishing results in the art of illuminating manuscripts as well as in embroidery and weaving. Genuine women far removed from unwomanly intellectualism, they knew how to handle not only the stylus but also the needle and the embroidery frame.

Of course, life in the convents of the island was not always idyllic. A number of abbesses had cares of all sorts, and many complaining letters went to Germany to the great friend of the nuns, St. Boniface. As an example, about the year 720 the Abbess Eangyth wrote him a long letter which gives us a glimpse into the soul of the troubled woman and also reveals that not a few shadows had fallen on the sunny landscape of these young Anglo-Saxon convents.

Eangyth groaned under the heavy burden of responsibility which rested on her as superior of a double monastery for nuns and monks. She tried to establish harmony among the members but did not succeed. The monks especially caused her grief. There were many quarrels. There were also difficulties from the outside. Her convent was poor, it held no great landed estates, and sometimes the necessities of life were missing. On top of that, the convent had to give contributions to the king, the queen, the bishop, the earls and other noblemen. To aggravate matters, the king was ill-disposed toward her. The good Abbess was accused in court by envious people, and so the king allowed the convent to feel his disfavor. She was almost alone in this world, as almost all her relatives had died. The only comfort remaining to her was her daughter Bugga.

She longed for peace and rest, and desired to make a pilgrimage to Rome to die at the grave of the apostles, the goal longed for by many Anglo-Saxons—kings no less than nuns. Urged by a feeling of solicitude and responsibility, Boniface protested against these pilgrimages of nuns to Rome, since a number of the nuns had succumbed to the dangers of the road.

That the old Germanic savagery would at times still assert itself in these English women, many of whom grew up within the shadow of the convent walls, is shown by an incident in the convent of Wimborne, where the young Lioba received her education.[1] Because of her severity, a certain prioress had made herself greatly disliked, especially among the young women of the convent. After her death and burial the young nuns trampled upon her grave with scornful shouts, to revenge themselves for the treatment which this prioress in her lifetime had meted out to them.

As we have already indicated, a large number of convents were founded during the seventh century in GAUL, the Frankish kingdom. Some of them followed the Rule of Caesarius, but a larger number bound themselves to the Irish observance. As the monasteries under the Rule of St. Columban had already adopted the Rule of St. Benedict in the seventh century, either making it the sole norm of their life or creating a new directive for their houses by combining the two rules, the convents did the same. These changed over entirely to the Rule of St. Benedict, and new foundations had the Rule from their beginning.

The most important Benedictine convents in France were Faremoutiers, Ste. Marie in Soissons, Rebais, Pavilly, St. Martial in Paris, Chelles and Jouarre. Numerous foundations were made within the solid walls of episcopal cities as a means of security. To name only a few, there were convents at Arles, Paris, Soissons, Poitiers, Marseille, Bourges, Autun, Lyons, Rheims, Troyes and Metz. As early as the seventh and eighth centuries there were convents in the country too, as at Baume-les-Dames, Remiremont, Mons, Maubeuge, Hasnon, Marchiennes and Nivelles.

In ITALY the eighth century was the period of foundations. The bishops and the secular grandees of the Lombard kingdom vied with one another in the erection of convents. In keeping with Italy's urban culture, the convents were founded almost exclusively in cities. Thus in the eighth century Brescia, Pavia,

---

[1] Translator's note: See Rudolf, Monk of Fulda, the Life of St. Leoba, *Anglo-Saxon Missionaries in Germany*, trans. and ed. by C. H. Talbot, New York, 1954, 203-226.

Milan, Venice, Bergamo, Turin, Cividata, Reggio, Ravenna, Piacenza, Ferrara, Florence, Lucca, Nepi, Capua and Naples had convents. Rome, the capital of Christendom, had 10 Benedictine convents in the ninth century.

The Italian convents were inferior to the convents of France and England in importance. They were purely contemplative institutes: participation in cultural or religious activities was out of the question, since conditions were very different from those in France and England.

About the year 700 the first convents according to the Rule of St. Benedict were established in GERMANY. Here, with very few exceptions, Benedictine missionaries founded convents in order to obtain the help and support of the nuns in the work of spreading the faith. The convent of Nonnberg in Salzburg may probably be considered Germany's oldest Benedictine convent. It was founded about the year 700 by St. Rupert († about 718), whose niece Ehrentrude became the first abbess. This foundation in Bavaria was followed by Kirchbach in 725 and Staffelsee in 739. Heidenheim was founded in 751 by St. Willibald, whose sister Walburga became the first abbess. Further foundations were Frauenwörth in Chiemsee, 782, and Karlsbach. In western Germany the two convents at Trier date from the eighth century: Oehren, which later changed its name to St. Irminen after the abbess Irmina († 708), and Pfalzel, whose Abbess Addula (Adela) was a friend of St. Boniface.

St. BONIFACE († 754) was the great promoter of Benedictine convents. It was through his efforts that the council of 742 obliged all convents to accept the Rule of St. Benedict and forbade all other rules. Lioba and her companions Kunihilt, Kunitrud and Thecla came from England in response to his call and transplanted the Anglo-Saxon traditions into the German convents: joy in mental work, a refined standard of life and receptivity to everything that is noble.

The convents of Tauberbischofsheim, Kitzingen, Ochsenfurt and Schornsheim are indebted to the activity of St. Boniface for their origin. They were all under the motherly care of St. Lioba, whose reputation in Germany matched that of the great Hilda in England. Her advice was listened to as eagerly in the court of Charlemagne as in the councils of bishops and abbots. These young convents vied with the monasteries in the work of permeating the German people with the Christian spirit. They transmitted the heritage of the faith to the women of the Carolingian era with the same enthusiasm with which they passed on the treasures of ancient civilization. Here also the nuns had the task of writing, studying and teaching. In the convent of Heidenheim the nun Hugburg wrote the life of St. Willibald and St. Wunibald, a work equal in value to those of the monks at that time.

The young Benedictine convents, associated with the monasteries and taking part in their work in one way or another, found a noteworthy parallel in the INSTITUTE OF CANONESSES soon after the year 800. The institute of consecrated virgins living in the world came to an end at this time. They were replaced by virgins living in a community, for whom the synod of Aachen in 817 set up a rule of life based on the old canons. The canonesses worked with the canons just as the nuns supported the work of the monks. Like the canons they held choir service in their institute churches, and they made provision for conducting divine services in their respective parish churches. They led a community life in their institutes under the guidance of an abbess. Their mode of life was somewhat mitigated, since they did not belong to the real ascetic state as the monks did. They were permitted to possess private property like the canons, they could have their own accommodations within the institute, and they could maintain a personal servant.

The institute of canonesses spread very fast, especially in Germany. Though found also in England, their real field of action was northern Germany. In the Ottonian era they made great progress, favored by the imperial house, which gave them princesses and royal widows as abbesses, so that they surpassed the convents in importance. Herford, Gandersheim and Quedlinburg were the most influential and powerful foundations. Henceforth both institutions developed side by side. The influence of the canonesses and the power of attraction which their institute possessed accounts for a slowing down in the foundation of new convents of nuns. Some districts of northern Germany for the time being had not a single convent according to the Rule of St. Benedict.

# CHAPTER 3

# FURTHER GROWTH OF BENEDICTINE
# CONVENTS

The collapse of the Carolingian empire, with its subsequent inner disorders and harassment by enemies from the outside, was not favorable to the erection of new convents. Records show the foundation of Andlau in Alsace in the year 884 through the beneficence of blessed Richardis, wife of Charles the Fat. Altenmünster in Mayence, St. Peter in Metz, and St. Mary in the capital, Cologne, may belong to the same period. About 986 Vilich at Bonn was founded; the saintly Abbess Adelaide (†about 1050), friend and counselor of St. Herbert of Cologne, was to shed a special lustre on it. The founding of Bergen on the Danube may also be of this period. In the eleventh century there were founded St. Walburg in Eichstätt (1035),[1] Göss in Styria (1004), Gurk (1043), renowned for its St. Hemma (†about 1045), Neuberg on the Danube and Kaufungen in Hessen, the foundation of the saintly Empress Kunigund.

The establishment of new convents reached its peak in the twelfth century. By that time the institute of canonesses had passed the peak of its development and had become a secular institute. The canonesses did not vow perpetual chastity; they were free to leave the institute at any time if they wished to marry. It is understandable that souls truly seeking God would no longer enter a chapter of canonesses. The religious zeal of the time, fostered by the monks of Cluny and Cîteaux, manifested itself remarkably in the foundation of convents. In the twelfth century

---

[1]Translator's note: See, The Nuns of St. Walburg, *Spring and Harvest, St. Walburg's Shrine: Symbol and Center of 900 Fruitful Years*, trans. by Sister Gonzaga Engelhart, O.S.B., St. Meinrad, Ind., 1952.

alone, Germany gained 100 new Benedictine convents, some of them in districts such as the diocese of Osnabrück where previously there had not been a single convent according to the Rule of St. Benedict. Among the new convents which achieved special distinction were Rolandswerth (before 1126), Gehrden (1135), Willebadessen (1149), Lippoldsberg (before 1100), as well as Bingen and Eibingen, the convents of St. HILDEGARD († 1179) on Rupertsberg, and Schönau, founded by St. ELIZABETH (†1164). The Netherlands saw the foundation of Egmond, Rynsburg, Siloe and Klaerwater, while Belgium added Messines and Forest.

In FRANCE also the Rule of St. Benedict spread. Whereas in the tenth century only 10 new foundations had been made, in the twelfth century more than 40 abbeys and a great number of priories were started. The convent of Marcigny, founded by St. Hugh of Cluny († 1109), achieved special importance and became the pattern for many convents.

In the ninth century the terrible catastrophe of the Danish invasion befell the convents of ENGLAND, suppressing them all except the one at Barking. Not until about the year 1100, during the reign of the Normans, were convents again restored. In the thirteenth century there were 12 abbeys and about 70 priories. The most important abbeys were Amesbury, Wilton, Barking and Shaftesbury.

The convents of SPAIN introduced the Rule of St. Benedict comparatively late. For the nuns of the Iberian peninsula the saintly Bishop Leander of Seville († 600) and the holy Archbishop Fructuosus († about 665) had written rules which were followed for a long time. Here the invasion of the Arabs and the establishment of Moorish control almost cut the peninsula off from the development taking place in the rest of Europe. Monachism therefore remained at the stage it had attained in the eighth century. This meant that the Rule of St. Benedict was known merely as a literary work in Spain; it did not penetrate into the convents of that country as a rule of life. Only about the year 1000 did it make its entrance as a rule to be lived. Perhaps the oldest Benedictine convent of Spain is San Pedro de las Puellas in Barcelona. This was followed by San Juan de las Abadessas and convents in Compostela, Gerona, Ona and San Miguel de Petrosa. From Spain, foundations were made in PORTUGAL, the earliest being San Pedro de Arouca and San Salvador de Vayrao.

While the Rule of St. Benedict was spreading in Spain and Portugal, the first Benedictine convents were established in the Slavic East. The oldest one in BOHEMIA is St. George in Prague. The first abbess of this royal abbey, Milada, daughter of Duke Boleslav I and sister of Boleslav II, received her consecration in Rome in 973 from Pope John XIII himself. This convent held a high place in the kingdom as a prince abbey, and the abbess along with the archbishop of Prague had the right to crown the queen. In the twelfth century the Rule of St. Benedict penetrated into POLAND, and in the thirteenth century Staniatki, Kulm and Lomza were the most important abbeys. Soon after the year 1000 DALMATIA and HUNGARY received their first convents.

After the year 1100 a large number of convents were founded in SCANDINAVIA. Among the 16 Benedictine convents in DENMARK were Hundslund, Randers, Wiborg, Dalum, Roskilde, Reinbeck and Holmen. SWEDEN had Borgö and St. Peter in Lund; whereas in NORWAY only the one at Selje in the diocese of Bergen is known. In distant ICELAND, Kirkjubaer was founded in 1186, followed by Ragnistadr in 1295.

Thus all countries of Western Christendom had convents according to the Rule of St. Benedict by the year 1200. Like the monasteries, they were most numerous and also most important in Germany and France.

The convents were autonomous and independent like the monasteries. If this was at times a drawback for the monasteries, it was a greater disadvantage for the convents. In their difficulties they were deprived of effective assistance, and they had no one to stimulate and advance them. Each abbess was dependent upon herself. Naturally, according to the general ecclesiastical custom, all convents had the bishop of the diocese as protector and visitator; but because of the great number of convents the bishop could not give as much attention to them as was necessary.

It is understandable that, in order to assure their temporal existence, preserve their religious spirit and persevere in their wholesome traditions, the convents sought to establish some kind of union, either among themselves or with the more firmly established monasteries. A council at Seville in the year 619 made the following ruling for the convents of Spain: "All convents should be under the administration and protection of the monks, who should care for them in spiritual as well as in temporal affairs."

However, this rule was not carried out everywhere, and the convents were left to themselves for the most part.

The desire for security in the temporal as well as the spiritual life gave rise to the DOUBLE MONASTERIES on Anglo-Saxon soil as early as the eighth century. In the course of time there were different forms of such double monasteries. The oldest form, the Anglo-Saxon, which was also imitated in France, comprised an abbey for women and one for men, both under the direction of an abbess. This type of convent did not last long and disappeared during the tenth century. A different type replaced this form whereby the abbey for monks attached a convent to itself and both groups were under the direction of the abbot. The nuns then served the monks by copying books and performing other services.

Such double monasteries sometimes developed very gradually. At first only one or the other woman recluse was permitted an enclosure near the church of the monastery. Then companions came to her, so that in time her cell became a small convent. Frequently the influx of women was so great that a special convent was established in the general vicinity of the monastery, which was often autonomous and only loosely connected with the monastery. These evolutionary steps can be clearly traced in the convent of Disibodenberg. St. Hildegard entered there at the time when a cell had expanded into a convent, which soon had so many nuns that she could draw upon them for a new foundation at Rupertsberg.

In Germany in the eleventh and twelfth centuries the abbeys for monks which granted a refuge or access to their churches were quite numerous. Among them were: St. Peter in Salzburg, Fulda, Engelberg, Petershausen, Schönau, Admont, St. Gall's, Lorsch, Lobbes, Liessies, Gellone and Afflighem. There were also such houses in England, as St. Alban's, and in France, as Molesme. Because of this union with the monasteries the nuns in such convents had economic security and also spiritual guidance. A *magistra* or *domina* ruled in the convent, but the real superior was the abbot who accepted the vows of the nuns. The profession formula in the convent at Admont under Abbot Godfrey I († 1165) reads: "I promise obedience to our Lord, to Abbot Godfrey and all who will rule after him, and stability to this convent of Admont and its saints until death, for the sake of eternal life."

This type of convent more or less renounced its independent existence, and the nuns accepted the task of simply serving the monks as sisters. It declined slowly from the beginning of the thirteenth century, and by the end of the fourteenth century there was hardly an abbey with a convent attached to it. Some convents became independent and located in other places. Others died out for want of new members, since admission to the Poor Clares and the Dominicans was now possible; or the monasteries no longer permitted convents to be attached to them.

During the period in which a large number of nuns were united with the monasteries of Germany, the double monasteries of the old Anglo-Saxon type were erected anew in France. These were founded no longer principally and purely for practical reasons, but from a religious motive, to portray the service which John tendered the Blessed Virgin Mary.

It was ROBERT of Arbrissel († 1117) who put this idea into practice and about 1090 founded the Order of FONTEVRAULT. All the convents of this Benedictine congregation were double monasteries in which the monks served the nuns and were under the government of the abbess. The monks bound themselves with the vow, "I promise to serve the handmaids of Christ until death with due respectful submission." All the convents of the union formed a congregation, at the head of which was the abbess of Fontevrault as superior general. The order spread quickly and soon became the most distinguished order in France. The nobility flocked to it in such great numbers that no other order had in its houses so many princesses from the most illustrious families of the kingdom. When Robert of Arbrissel died the order already numbered 3000 nuns and monks, and the mother abbey alone had 300 nuns.

These double monasteries were a monastic type portraying interdependence of the nuns and monks. They emphasized particularly the assistance given to the nuns on the part of the monks.

It was inevitable that the great monastic movements of the eleventh century, Cluny and its branches, which desired the renewal of monasticism, should also be interested in the convents, and that the revival of the religious life in the monasteries should also affect the convents. Since most of these monastic movements had the further objective of leading the monasteries out of their isolation and giving them stronger support by uniting them into a central unit, this objective also redounded to the good of the convents. The convents needed such protection even more than the monasteries did.

It was St. Hugh († 1109), first abbot of Cluny, who incorporated a convent into the Cluniac family under the same conditions as the monasteries. About 1061 he founded the convent of Marcigny. He built the church and the convent and cared for everything the convent needed. With tender fatherly care he took charge of the young foundation and appointed the monk Rencho as spiritual director to give the nuns "the nourishment of the divine word." The convent received the constitution and customs of the monastery of Cluny, which meant that the life of divine service—the psalmody with its votive offices, processions and other ceremonials—constituted the order of the day and year.

After Marcigny came other convents, like Grelonge-Salles, Montchal, Laveine, Feldbach in Alsace, Istein and Sölden in the diocese of Constance, and many others in Italy, Spain and England. In accordance with the Cluniac constitution, most of the convents were only priories. Their real superior was the abbot of Cluny, who appointed a prior as his representative in the convent. The prior represented the convent in external affairs and had charge of temporalities. The abbot of Cluny also appointed the abbess or prioress of the convent, who was entrusted with the direction of the community of nuns. Thus the individual convents had no autonomy, remaining completely under the authority of the abbot of Cluny, who made the visitations of the convent and whose regulations the convent had to follow.

In the eleventh century in Italy there was a Cluniac center, the abbey of Fruttuaria, which also took an interest in convents. Although spiritually it was completely influenced by Cluny, it did not form any strong union, but contented itself with arranging the regular life in agreement with its own customs for the convents united to it. Since these customs were brought to Germany by the monasteries of St. Blaise and Siegburg, the usages of Fruttuaria made their entrance into many German convents also and effected a renewal of the religious life. They were established, for example, in the convents of Berau, Muri, Fahr and Donauwörth.

More significant in Germany than the movement of Fruttuaria was the reform which started from the monastery of Hirsau in the Black Forest. The reform was closely connected with that of Cluny and reached about 100 monasteries in the north as well as in the south of Germany. Since many of the monasteries that joined the Hirsau movement had a convent attached to them or dependent on them, it was understandable that the Hirsau observance also penetrated numerous convents.

The customs of the Hirsau monastery were introduced into the monastery at Admont about the year 1090, and transmitted at once to the convent. From here they were then transmitted to Kirchheim, to St. George on the Längsee, Neuburg and Bergen on the Danube, and from there to Odilienberg in Alsace. Likewise, the monastery of St. George in the Black Forest brought the Hirsau observance to Amtenhausen, Gebweiler, Friedensweiler and Graufthal in Alsace. Furthermore, we find the Hirsau customs at Fischbach, Kemnade, Altdorf, Klein-Komburg, Frauenalb, Schönau, and also at Rupertsberg.

Archbishop Conrad I of Salzburg († 1147) proved himself a great friend of the convents during the twelfth century. Through his efforts the regular life flourished in Chiemsee, Berchtesgaden, St. Zeno in Reichenhall and other convents.

We learn something about the observance in a Hirsau convent from the profession of vows of the abbesses and nuns in the convent of Lippoldsberg on the Weser. They accepted the customs of Hirsau about the year 1100.

The manner of observing the enclosure received special consideration. Only those who have the permission of the confessor or the community may carry a key. The confessor may enter the convent only to visit the sick and to accompany guests. Guests are led into the chapter room to transact their business, but whatever business can be dispatched quickly should be done at the chapter-window. If guests wish to see the convent or the workshops, they are permitted to look into the rooms, but they may not tarry there. The abbess may leave the convent if a need arises and then only with a companion.

The convent shall always have a capable confessor. The selection is made by the five neighboring abbots, who also determine his rights in detail. One of these is that, with the consent of a majority of the nuns, he may advise the abbess to resign the government of the convent in the event that she has not discharged her duties well.

Special fast days are the vigils of St. George, St. Peter's Chains, St. Nicholas and St. Mary Magdalen. Days of abstinence are Mondays, Wednesdays and Fridays unless they happen to be feast days. The nuns are required to sew their own clothing as hand work. Their garb should be similar to that of the monks with the exception that they wear a veil instead of the cowl. The abbess is not permitted to have her own residence or her own table nor to keep maids for her service.

All these convents, whether they followed Cluny, Fruttuaria, Hirsau or any other strong center, received stability in their religious life by having a regular observance to direct their community life. The abbesses did not have to search for a specific form of observance, since it was given to them. All the convents, through this similarity of observance, formed a spiritual union which gave support to community life. Almost everywhere they had a monk of the same observance as their spiritual director. Even if not all of them were subject to an abbot as their guide and visitor, as were those in the Cluny congregation, still they ordinarily looked to an abbey of monks as their intellectual and spiritual mainstay.

The twelfth century also saw, however, an alliance of convents in which the aim was to strengthen themselves by entering into a union with one another as convents.

One of the first attempts of this kind was the Congregation of the PARACLETE. The celebrated teacher and monk Abelard († 1142) had his student Héloïse brought to the convent of the Paraclete in the diocese of Troyes when she had to leave Argenteuil. He himself developed the statutes for the convent.[2] The convent progressed very satisfactorily under the direction of the highly gifted Héloïse; other convents, such as Pommeraie, Treinel and Laval, accepted its statutes; and a congregation of convents was formed under the rule of the abbess of the Paraclete.

Other congregations followed this pattern of union, as for instance the congregation formed by the convent of ST. SULPICE DE LA FORÊT, which comprised numerous houses, mainly priories, in Brittany, Anjou and Touraine. The congregations of convents, like the congregations of monasteries, held annual general chapters at which the superiors of the various convents had to render an account of their administration.

[2] Migne 178, 255 ff.

In ITALY a similar congregation of nuns was started in the thirteenth century, the Congregation of the Handmaids of the Virgin Mary. The first convent of this union was founded in 1258 by Santucce of Terrabotti († 1305) in GUBBIO. It accepted the observance which Abbot Sperandeus of Gubbio († before 1264) had given to his monastery. The abbess of Gubbio was the leader of the union, to which 25 convents soon belonged. She appointed abbesses or prioresses in the various houses, presided at the general chapter, and also held the visitation in the different houses. From 1306 on, the central convent of the congregation was St. Anna's in Rome (Santa Anna de' Funari).

The great question which the convents of the Middle Ages had to face was how to assure their very existence in the face of demands from secular powers and also of economic difficulties. Very closely connected with this was the question of spiritual and cultural direction. Both of these were best guaranteed by uniting with monasteries or by forming a closer bond among themselves.

The second question about which the convents were concerned was how the life within the house should be regulated, for the Rule of St. Benedict gives only general directions for many things and leaves numerous details to the discretion of the abbot. Moreover, everyday living with its changing conditions always brought up new questions for consideration. It was not given to every abbess to make a correct choice in these matters and to arrange everything so as to meet the spirit of the Rule and the approved traditions of monasticism.

For the formation of the domestic life the customs of Cluny and the other great Cluniac abbeys offered the needed concrete help to the convents. Most convents of the eleventh and twelfth centuries lived in the spirit of Cluny; that is, the life was determined not so much by the letter of the Rule of St. Benedict but rather by the customs, which were far removed from the letter of the old Benedictine law. The Cluny ideal stressed the importance of choir prayer, to which almost the entire day was devoted, so that the convents which followed this usage, in contrast to the Anglo-Saxon and early German convents, devoted only a small amount of time to work. To be a nun meant to perform community prayer. In addition to the psalmody, many extra prayers had been added, especially numerous intercessions for the

living and still more for the deceased. Wherever it was possible
two Masses were said daily: the early Mass, which was a votive
Mass or a Mass for the deceased, and the Mass of the day after
Terce.

In another aspect of their development, the convents had ac-
quired great and widely scattered possessions, and had to take
part in many mundane affairs. Abbesses, like abbots, played a
role in the feudal state systems; and the convents, as owners of
estates or even of small principalities, had taken governmental
duties upon themselves. In some convents there was scarcely a
trace left of the retirement from the world and the peaceful life
in seclusion. The nuns were in no way worldly, nor had they
ceased to strive for perfection; but the entire structure of the
convents, especially their association with the world, had drawn
the nuns far from what was once understood as a monastic life.

At the beginning of the twelfth century, the voice of CISTER-
CIANISM was raised against this evolution that had brought the
monks and nuns into close contact with the world. Fired by holy
zeal for the true ideal of the Rule of St. Benedict, the leaders and
the followers, above all ST. BERNARD of Clairvaux († 1153), became
the champions of pure Benedictinism, which would conform to
the Rule and not the customs.

The fathers of Cîteaux recognized Benedictinism as retirement
from the world, solitude, poverty and manual work. They did
not approve of great, widely-dispersed possessions, and numerous
estates on which bondsmen or tenants worked for the members
of the convent, but rather they would have only so much property as was necessary to maintain life. Above all, simplicity and
poverty should prevail in the house as well as in the church. The
convent should be located, not on the highways nor on the heights
to be seen from afar, but rather in solitary, quiet valleys where it
will not be disturbed by streams of visitors. In general all ties with
the world should be dissolved, particularly with the feudal state
to which so many Benedictine convents belonged.

Most significant, however, was the Cistercians' monastic ideal
properly so called, which stood in sharp contrast to that of Cluny.
The Cistercian ideal of piety was not the continual and solemn
celebration of the liturgy. In conformity with the Rule, the day
was allotted to work and reading, interrupted only by the three
Little Hours, each of which lasted a mere 10 minutes. Thus the

psalmody was curtailed, and all the additions that had accumulated in the course of time were dropped. This again allowed the monk and also the nun some spare time during the day, which had no longer been given them in the Cluniac houses, since they spent almost the entire day in choir. Manual work was again restored to honor. The time free from choir prayer was devoted to manual work, to private mental prayer, to mystic contemplation of the mysteries of faith, and to further spiritual development through reading and through listening to the conferences of the spiritual director. The aim of the young Cistercian order was not the practice of extraordinary austerities but a true spiritual life in close union with the Rule of St. Benedict and a loving piety of the heart. It is understandable that this ideal found enthusiastic reception among women.

Here they found everything over which so many convents were concerned: through union with the young community of Cistercians they had strong support; through the yearly general chapter of the order they had secure guidance; through the abbot under whom they were placed by the general chapter they had strong and trustworthy direction in temporal as well as in spiritual affairs. Furthermore, the Cistercian ideal of piety with its tendency to mystic life and to a more personal form of prayer had great appeal to the hearts of women.

Many convents were united with Cîteaux. These convents were not, as were those united to Cluny, subordinate simply to a central house, but rather each individual convent was assigned to a father-abbot who had to assume the care and responsibility of it. He appointed one of his monks as spiritual director, made the visitations of the convent, provided for it, and saw to it that the decrees of the general chapter were observed. According to the Cistercian ideal he did not have dominion over the convent but rather a custody based on love. Some abbots were entrusted with several convents, as was the abbot of the large monastery of Eberbach in the Rhineland. He was the father-abbot for 20 convents. The abbesses themselves did not take part in the general chapters of the order but were represented there by the spiritual director, who bore the title of prior.

The impetus to Cistercianism was so strong among the nuns that the general chapter at the beginning of the thirteenth century forbade further acceptance of convents into the order because the monasteries had become too heavily burdened with their care. One reason for this condition was that bishops zealous for souls would often order that a Benedictine convent be admitted into the Cistercian union, because they saw therein a guarantee for good discipline. Thus Archbishop Siegfried III of Mayence in 1243 arranged the incorporation of Allenmünster in Mayence and shortly thereafter of Dalheim in the Rhineland into the Cistercian order and entrusted their care to the abbot of Eberbach. Hoven near Zülpich joined of its own accord.

The enthusiasm of the nuns for Cistercianism was not diminished by the prohibition of the general chapter against accepting any more convents into the order. Many Benedictine nuns adopted the Cistercian way of life without being accepted into the order. They took the white habit of the Cistercians and followed their observances. They regarded as their spiritual father St. Bernard, the master of the mystical life, who through his exposition of the Canticle of Canticles had shown the nuns the way of the bride to the Beloved. The convent of Helfta, for example, in the thirteenth century accepted the Cistercian customs without belonging to the order. In a similar way many convents in the eleventh and twelfth centuries had accepted the customs of Cluny without belonging to the congregation.

The number of Cistercian convents soon exceeded the number of Benedictine convents. Thus Germany in the fifteenth century had 115 Benedictine convents and 220 according to the order of Cîteaux. The Cistercian movement brought a wonderful impetus to the religious life, and even the Benedictine nuns of the old observance were not untouched by the stream that had its source in Cîteaux.

# CHAPTER 4

# LIFE IN A BENEDICTINE CONVENT
# OF THE EARLY MIDDLE AGES

The legal position held by a Benedictine convent in the organism of the state or the Church in the Middle Ages showed wide variation according to circumstances. On the SPIRITUAL SIDE, convents were naturally under the supervision of the bishop in whose diocese they were located, in accordance with the traditions of the early Church. The bishop had the right to make the visitation of the convent, to consecrate the abbess and the nuns, and he also had the right of "guesting." This meant that he could take up quarters for the night at the convent with his entire retinue, horsemen, horses and all. The fact that the convent then had to provide for him as well as for his servants and horses imposed a heavy financial burden on poor convents.

Since the economic status of a number of convents in the later Middle Ages was not good, they sought exemption from "guesting." An exemption was seldom granted to the monasteries except to the most outstanding ones like Fulda, Cluny and Monte Cassino; and it was granted even more rarely to convents. They were entirely under the spiritual control of the bishop, who could even give them directions for their conventual life and who often installed the abbess or removed her from office according to his own judgment.

Besides the bishop, many convents also recognized a second spiritual authority, the abbot of the monastery on which they were dependent either by their foundation or by a later development.

The SECULAR POSITION of the convent was generally determined by the manner of its founding. If the king established the convent, it was a royal convent, in Germany and Italy an IMPERIAL CONVENT, the king or the emperor respectively being its highest protector. From small estates these convents grew into territories over which the abbess, like an imperial abbot, ruled. She had charge over the convent property and its members in place of the emperor. The great recognition which such a convent received and the position of power which it occupied were dearly bought, of course: the convent had not the right to vote; the emperor appointed the abbess according to his own judgment, leaving the nuns only the right to nominate. Furthermore, the convent had to pay taxes to the emperor, and among other things it was obliged to equip completely for army service a prescribed number of soldiers.

Many of these imperial convents were later elevated to prince abbeys, the princess abbess having the sovereign rights as well as a seat in the *Reichstag*. Prominent prince abbeys in Germany were Regensburg, Burtscheid at Aachen, and Frauenwörth. Other convents which did not attain to imperial rank were nevertheless members of the provincial diet, and as such held a prominent place in the country to which they belonged.

Already in the Anglo-Saxon era and also in the early German period, the majority of the nuns belonged to the nobility. The elevation to imperial convents or further to prince abbeys led many convents to accept only the nobility, and in some instances only such as belonged to high nobility. In the eleventh and especially in the twelfth century, many other convents outside of this class declared themselves monasteries for the nobility, MONASTERIA NOBILIA. When Abbot Hugh of Cluny founded the convent of Marcigny, he established it only for the daughters of nobility. The convent of St. Hildegard at Rupertsberg was another one open only to the nobility.

Even in pious circles this gave no offense. In fact, when the abbess of the Augustinian convent, St. Thomas near Andernach, appealed to St. Hildegard on this matter and asked about the justification of such a convent, Hildegard replied, "The lower class (meaning commoners and peasants) should not elevate itself above the higher. What man gathers all his livestock—oxen, sheep, donkeys and goats—into one barn without harm? Therefore also (in the convent) there should be segregation, lest the different types brought together into one fold be affected by feelings of superiority or of inferiority, but especially lest their in-grained sensibilities be offended and they grate on one another, those of the higher rank abusing the lower, or the latter attempt-ing to elevate themselves to the higher."

Alongside the imperial or royal convents stood the great body of DEPENDENT CONVENTS that had an overlord or proprietor other than the emperor or king. The proprietor—it was usually the founder or his heir or legal successor—could be the pope, a bishop, a duke, a count, an abbot, or the city council, or even an ab-bess, whether it was a convent or any other institution.

For all these dependent convents as well as for the imperial convents there existed a council, which made its influence felt either through an administrator, as in the imperial convents, or directly. Influence was exerted in the election of the abbess, in the reception of novices and in the administration of property.

The movements of Cluny in France and Hirsau in Germany fought for the freedom of their monasteries and independence from overseers and proprietors; but the convents were not always able to defend themselves against the lords, especially since the rights of these lords were often stated in the foundation charter.

At the head of the abbey was the ABBESS, a title for the superior of a convent which can be traced to the beginning of the sixth century. During the Middle Ages the names *domina* and *ma-gistra* appeared frequently, the name "deaconess" for an abbess having gone out of use since the eighth century.

As we have already said, hardly a single convent had a free election from the Carolingian era until the Hirsau congregation fought for it again. The abbess was almost always appointed, and it often happened that a nun was appointed who was not a mem-ber of the convent, or even of the order, or that a widow belonging to the laity was appointed, and pronounced her vows only at her consecration as abbess. Often enough young girls who were still in their adolescence were chosen. Abbesses of 20 years of age were not rare, and we hear of such as were only 12 years old. In 1059 Urraca, daughter of King Ramiros I, became an abbess at the age of 11, having entered the convent of Séros in Aragon at the age of nine. That the choice of a young abbess was not always unfortunate is shown at Helfta, where Gertrude of Hackeborn was appointed to this office at the age of 19 and performed the duties of an ab-bess most satisfactorily for 40 years, from 1251 to 1291.

As a mark of distinction, the abbess of the Middle Ages carried only the staff. A special ring and pectoral cross for an abbess are a later custom in imitation of the pontifical insignia of abbots.

Under the management of the abbess the other officials performed the conventual duties of administration entrusted to them. Next to the abbess was the prioress, also called provost (*praeposita*) or dean, after whom in the larger convents came the subprioress. Then followed the cellarer, who had charge of providing necessary food for the convent, and the mistress of the wardrobe, who had charge of the clothing.

The chantress was important; generally only one who had been especially trained would be chosen. She was not only, as today, a director of the choir but, since there was much room for development in the liturgical life, she was expected to compose hymns and set them to music. Thus she had to be both poet and musician at the same time. Since the library consisted principally of liturgical hymns, she was ordinarily librarian also. Under her direction the copying and illustrating of manuscripts was carried on in the scriptorium. Next in line were the portress, the sacristan, the treasurer and the almoner.

The infirmarian also played an important role. She, like the chantress, required special training. She not only took care of the sick but was also physician and pharmacist in the convent. What remained of the art and knowledge of the medical science of antiquity was preserved and propagated only in the religious houses, especially in the convents. Every convent had its own herb-garden from which potions and poultices could be made; and we know from a nun like St. Hildegarde what extensive knowledge of the art of healing still prevailed in the convents of the twelfth century.

Finally, to instruct the children who came as oblates, every convent had a teacher, a *magistra,* to whom assistants were given if needed. "Outside" schools generally were conducted only by canonesses, while the nuns in their schools instructed only the girls who belonged to the convent. The convent schools were always well provided for, and if at any time a qualified teacher was not available in the convent, a monk or secular priest or even a lay person was engaged as teacher. The subjects taught were Latin, writing, reading, music and womanly handwork.

During this period members for the convent were recruited almost entirely from the higher classes, the nobility or the descendants of knights and patricians. A further characteristic of the times was that most of the nuns entered the convent as mere children, ranging in age from 6 to 8 years, sometimes as young as 4 years, as was the case with Gertrude of Helfta. Many were even promised to God before birth.

This practice was thought compatible with the times and seemed preferable to the exercise of free choice in later years. The oblation on the part of the parents was considered binding. According to a decree of a Spanish synod these children were not required to make a profession of vows, since they were already bound by the promise of their parents. Profession usually did take place, however, at about the fifteenth year of age. These children received their training and education in the convent and participated in the choir service, at least during the daytime. They were representative of the cultured class in the convent.

Besides these a smaller group comprised those who came to the convent later in life, mostly as widows. In the Middle Ages there were few nuns who entered the convent by a completely free decision at the age of 20 to 25, as most do today. The result of a visitation in the convent of Niedermünster in Regensburg in 1246 shows that practically all the nuns had come to the convent as children.

Consequently the medieval convents did not have a novitiate as we have today. The oblates required no probationary period since they were already bound by their oblation, and the few who came at a mature age were almost always permitted to pronounce their vows after a period of four weeks. This was the custom in all the convents of Cluny. The opinion was prevalent that anyone who had fled from the world should not again be exposed to its dangers. Thus our present concept of a vocation was sadly lacking. As a consequence, in the late Middle Ages hardly any of those living in the convents had a true vocation to the religious life. At a time when religion was in the ascendancy, such a system did not offer any particular danger, but no one stopped to think that it was decidedly contrary to the Rule of St. Benedict. The usages had sanctioned this and many other practices.

From the institute of consecrated virgins the nuns took over the ceremony of the CONSECRATION OF VIRGINS, and in the early

Middle Ages it was conferred in many convents. Because of the great number of convents and the great number of nuns in each convent, it was naturally quite a burden for the bishop to go to every convent for this particular ceremony. Hence it became the custom that the consecration of virgins, no longer connected with the ceremony of profession, took place according to the canonical decrees at the age of maturity, whereas profession could be made early in life. The bishop conferred the consecration when he came to the convent either for the consecration of a church or for a visitation; then all the nuns were consecrated, sometimes 60 at a time.

Profession was received by the abbess. It was a simple rite, as prescribed by the Rule of St. Benedict and the customs of Cluny, Hirsau and other monasteries. In later times when the consecration of virgins was resumed, the profession ceremony was incorporated into the rite of consecration of virgins. After the middle of the twelfth century the consecration of virgins was discontinued. The new orders were not acquainted with it. The canonesses omitted it and thereby influenced also the customs of the Benedictine convents.

The number of nuns in the convents naturally varied in the individual houses according to their prominence and prestige and also according to their economic potentialities. In the Anglo-Saxon and Carolingian times some convents had a great many members: there were some with 100, even with 300 and as many as 500 nuns. In the course of time the numbers kept decreasing. In the eleventh and twelfth centuries a decrease was due to the fact that besides the Benedictine convents there were a large number of convents of other orders, such as Cistercian, Augustinian and Premonstratensian. Then, too, some convents accepted as members only women of noble birth and sometimes of only the highest nobility.

In the twelfth century a convent of 60 nuns was thought to be large, but most of the convents had scarcely half that number. In view of the limited means of support, the number of nuns in a convent of this era was restricted to 25 by the bishop or the convent officials, and this number was scarcely ever exceeded. Some of the building plans, which are still available, and also the size of the nuns' churches, indicate that the convents were not very large.

As directed by the Rule of St. Benedict, the nuns themselves in the earliest period, like the monks, performed all the domestic WORK in the kitchen, the bakery, the various shops and the garden. Work and prayer alternated with each other throughout the day. But the more the choir service was spread out according to the reform of Benedict of Aniane († 821) and especially that of Cluny, the less time there remained for the performance of menial tasks. The daughters of the nobility were loathe to do work which was ordinarily done by servants in the world. Already as early as the Carolingian period, menial work was gradually transferred to maid servants, while in the monasteries it was performed by vassals and servants.

Influenced by the Cistercians, who tolerated no lay servants in the monastery but accepted lay brothers instead, the nuns also accepted lay sisters to do the menial work for the convent. Originally these sisters, like the lay brothers in the monasteries, were not religious. They made the vow of obedience to the abbess and they bound themselves to work. Many convents also had lay brothers to do the field work, and they, like the lay sisters, merely promised obedience to the convent and generally lived outside the convent proper, on the convent farms. The number of lay sisters was at first very small and remained so until the eighteenth century.

Like the monasteries the convents lived from the produce of their estates. These represented widely dispersed farms with meadows, woods, fields, vineyards, and ponds or streams, which were leased to servants, tenants or vassals who paid the rent to the convent. For its own management the convent had no farm, only a vegetable garden on the convent grounds and perhaps an orchard, tended by the nuns themselves. The larger their possessions, the larger and more certain was the income; therefore every provident abbess naturally strove to preserve the possessions of the convent or to increase them. An administrator, who was usually the provost of the convent, had charge of the community property, while the procurator managed the individual farms.

The PROVOST was first and foremost the spiritual father of the convent. He was usually a monk of a monastery in some way affiliated with the convent, but sometimes he was a secular priest, if the nuns could not secure a monk. Generally he had a vicar as his assistant, and both lived either in a room near the convent entrance or in a special house.

The provost was the spiritual director of the nuns as well as the confessor. He offered Mass and administered the sacraments to them. It was not always easy to find the right person for this position, and we read that St. Hildegard had reason to complain about the "unreliability of the priests." The provost was also the legal adviser for the convent and with the abbess and community took care of all business matters. He countersigned all documents, and through him all legal business had to be transacted, all buying, selling, exchange, or mortgage of property. Often he had a voice in the election of the abbess.

This arrangement may have been helpful in normal times; but in times of religious and economic depression it caused great difficulty and was a source of strife and annoyance. Often the provost neglected his duties as overseer. Sometimes he did not give the nuns the rent due them but appropriated it to himself. The convents then agreed to allot a definite income to the provost out of which he had to defray his personal expenses. He had a right only to his salary as provost.

The arrangement which St. Hildegard made for Rupertsberg, when she separated her convent from the monastery of Disibodenberg, illustrates the legal aspects of founding a convent in the Middle Ages. The convent should be free in every respect. It should be simply under the protectorate of the archbishop of Mayence and never have an overseer other than the archbishop. No lay person should have any right whatsoever over the convent. Toward the monastery of Disibodenberg, there should be a relation of dependence only in so far as the nuns were to receive advice in spiritual matters and on questions of observance and conventual life from there rather than elsewhere. For divine services, they should request priests from this monastery too, with full freedom to select one agreeable to them. The monks of Disibodenberg should have no rights whatsoever over the possessions of the convent of Rupertsberg.

When the early virgins patterned their lives and ascetic practices on those of the monks, they retired into solitude, and it was a concern of the monks from the very beginning to preserve for these nuns that seclusion from the world which would be conducive to a life of prayer and dedication to divine service in all purity of heart. This gave rise to the ENCLOSURE in nuns' convents. As we have already mentioned, St. Caesarius in his rule for the city convent at Arles included the precept of strict enclosure for the nuns. Other city convents in France which accepted his rule naturally took over also the precept of strict enclosure.

This form of strict enclosure was not accepted at first by the nuns of the Anglo-Saxon island. For one thing, it had no basis in the Rule of St. Benedict; and moreover it was not compatible with the position held by a woman in Germanic society, especially a woman of noble family. We even hear of double monasteries between which communication was carried on through a window, but this was due to special circumstances brought about by the close proximity of monks and nuns. Aside from this, however, we do hear that abbesses appeared before the synods and that nuns undertook pilgrimages to Rome, so that enclosure behind grate and curtain was out of the question.

Rudolph of Fulda (†865) informs us that in the convent of Wimborne in Lioba's time "no one could go out unless she could give a good reason or a need for doing so." Lioba and her companions brought this tradition to Germany. Lioba herself traveled to the imperial palace to see her friend, Empress Hildegard; she visited her convents and the grave of her fatherly friend and relative, Boniface.

Originally, enclosure for the nuns was not stricter than for the monks, yet greater reserve was expected from women than from men. In the city convents of western France it was the custom for the nuns to leave their convents on the feast day of the patron of their cathedral church, not only to say a short prayer in the church of the saint or at his grave, but also to sing the Office in his honor. We meet with other cases in the tenth century where nuns who themselves had a highly honored saint, set out on a tour carrying the shrine of their saint through the countryside, either to further devotion to him or to collect alms for their convent so that they could rebuild and refurnish a church and convent ravaged by fire or plunder.

When nuns were forbidden to ride horseback or to go on a journey, as St. Hugh decreed at the foundation of Marcigny, a reason was given: there are certain dangers that threaten a woman, who, unlike a man, cannot defend herself against attack nor easily find a hiding place.

For the nuns of the Middle Ages there was of course no unrestrained freedom, which would have been contrary to the spirit of the monastic life and also to the good breeding of a noble woman, who appeared in public very seldom. The enclosure, however, was not comparable to that of the recluses, who allowed themselves to be locked in a cell and had communication with the world only through a window. Monastic enclosure allowed St. Hildegard to travel: she was seen in Cologne, Trier, Metz, Würzburg and Bamberg and stayed at many convents. Abbesses traveled to the imperial and legislative assemblies and the provincial chapter, inspected the convent property and transacted business with the bishop or in the city.

To be sure, repeated objections were raised against this practice of traveling, which, as we shall see later, led to grave abuses. Through a general church law Pope Boniface VIII enacted the strict enclosure,[1] but this law was not observed in Germany. In the Romanic countries, however, such as Italy and Spain, where women were more domestic, strict enclosure was kept. But in Germany even the reforms of the fifteenth century, which introduced the enclosure, permitted journeys for valid reasons, especially to attend chapter meetings on the business of reform. When the abbot of Eberbach, about the middle of the fifteenth century, issued new statutes for the 20 convents under his jurisdiction, he allowed the nuns, for a legitimate reason and with permission, to go on a journey, even to visit relatives.

Conventual daily life was determined first of all by the Rule of St. Benedict, which was read daily in chapter. How highly it was treasured is indicated by the fact that the nuns translated it into the vernacular. Still extant, for example, is a German translation from a convent in the middle Rhineland.[2] Along with the Rule, the customs were to be observed.[3] As already stated, the liturgical life, consisting of the celebration of the canonical hours and accompanying devotions, held first place in the horarium of the nuns. About midnight, in some convents before midnight, the nuns rose for Matins, then retired for rest, to rise again at about 6 o'clock and begin the day Office. About 6 o'clock in the

---

[1] Translator's note: See Rev. Garrett Francis Barry, O.M.I., *Violation of the Cloister*, Washington 1942.

[2] E. Sievers, *Die Oxforder Benediktinerregel*, Halle 1887.

[3] Neues Archiv der Gesellschaft für ältere deutsche Gesch. 27, 1902, 656-669.

evening the nuns' day generally came to an end. People of the
Middle Ages retired early.

The nuns' choir was located in front of the altar in early times;
by the early Middle Ages, however, it had already been transferred to the upper church, either to the gallery or, in a double
church like Schwarzrheindorf, to the upper story. The gallery in
the rear of the nave was generally the place of the nuns, while
the servants occupied the nave. In some churches the nuns' sec-
tion was not confined to the west or rear gallery; a three-winged
gallery covered the whole church, including the side aisles. The
west side of the church was reserved exclusively for the convent
and thus closed to lay people. The vault under it often served as
a tomb, so that the choir prayers and supplications for the deceased were held over their very bodies.

As the Rule of St. Benedict prescribed, the nuns slept in common dormitories. Individual cells first appeared in the fifteenth
century. In general the nuns spent their time during the day in
the cloisters. Reading was done in carrels or niches along the
cloisters and dormitories. There was a separate scriptorium for
the scribes and copyists; in winter they used a common calefac-
tory.

Zealous abbesses encouraged study among the nuns. Abbess
Gertrude of Hackeborn († 1292) at Helfta maintained that when
zeal for study wanes and an understanding of Holy Scripture
is lacking, the spiritual life declines. Therefore, she was indefatig-
able in her efforts to procure books, which she purchased or bor-
rowed to be copied. The most highly educated of her nuns was
the chantress Mechtild of Wippra († 1299).

Helfta's fame is assured for all time by three nuns: Mechtild
of Magdeburg († 1282), who spent the last 12 years of her life at
Helfta and there completed her work "The Flowing Light of
the Godhead";[4] Mechtild of Hackeborn († 1298), author of a
book on grace; and Gertrude the Great († 1302), who gave us
her mystical experiences in "Herald of Divine Love."[5] Whoever
reads these descriptions of the life at Helfta and of the nuns and
the brothers who served them, cannot fail to get the impression
that here was once a paradise on earth.

[4]Trans. by Lucy Menzies, London 1953.
[5]Translator's note: See *The Life and Revelations of St. Gertrude,* Westminster,
Md. 1949.

Even if original authorship was the exception, yet reading, writing and study were generally fostered. The high standards of culture and education in a convent of the Middle Ages are revealed to us in the writings of St. Hildegard. She, like Gertrude and Mechtild at Helfta, was educated in a convent school which imparted not only theological and ascetical knowledge but also a great deal of secular knowledge, including the natural sciences, astronomy and medicine.

Of the nuns of the Middle Ages St. Hildegard is probably the most outstanding in her accomplishment of combining theological training with secular knowledge. She portrayed her theologically and liturgically formed piety in vivid word-pictures which made a strong impression on her contemporaries. Moreover, she carried on a correspondence with all her contemporaries of rank and importance and everywhere was considered as an oracle in matters both spiritual and temporal. Less accomplished was Elizabeth of Schönau († 1165), but she was also held in high esteem.

The exterior life of the nuns admitted of no particular austerities because the Rule of St. Benedict does not provide for them. Rising at night, frequent fasts, and abstinence from meat were penances that were practiced by many lay people also and were not considered as particularly ascetic. The monotony of life was broken by the many feast days of the Middle Ages, which according to the customs of Cluny were always celebrated with special delicacies at table. There was also the customary relaxation three or four times a year in connection with bloodletting.[6] For this, one retired to the infirmary for some days, did not take part in choir service, received more nourishing food, including meat, and had a sort of vacation.

The religious life consisted first and foremost in the performance of choir service, which was given particular solemnity through the procession in the cloister and other practices. As we have said, two Masses were celebrated daily in the convents. The nuns generally went to confession every two weeks, even though they received the holy Eucharist only once a month, usually on the first Sunday. If there happened to be one of the greater

---

[6]Translator's note: Apparently during the Middle Ages great importance was attached to regular bloodletting or bleeding several times a year. A bloodletting calendar was made out which showed the points of election under the various signs of the Zodiac. The process was simple, so that a monk performed it in the monastery and undoubtedly a nun in the convent.

feasts during the month, they received their monthly Communion on this feast day. This was also customary in the monasteries. It sprang from the high regard during the Middle Ages for the Eucharist, which was approached only with the greatest reserve.

Charity was practiced most zealously in the convents. The poor found shelter there, as did also the sick and feeble. Many convents kept a home for old people or a shelter for pilgrims nearby. It was the custom of almost all convents that the poor were remembered with special alms on specified days, such as the anniversaries of deceased abbesses. Whoever needed a potion or some salve received it from the convent, and there also he received advice on all ailments.

The convents of the Benedictine nuns were at this time flourishing strongholds of the spiritual life. This lasted with short interruptions from the eighth to the middle of the thirteenth century. They gave a meaning to the lives of many women of the Middle Ages which far surpassed the intellectual level of a woman of the middle class or even of a lady at court.

Wilbert of Gembloux († 1204), who had spent three years in the convent of St. Hildegard at Rupertsberg, gave a report in a letter to his confrere Bovo on the life of the nuns, applicable also to other convents:

"It is so wonderful to observe here the contest in striving for virtue, with what affection the mother loves her daughters and with what respect the daughters submit to the mother! It is impossible to say whether the mother or the daughters excel. For these holy handmaids of God are so eager to serve God, to guard themselves, to honor and obey one another that one can easily see in them how with the help of Christ the weaker sex has conquered over self, the world and the devil.

"On feast days the nuns sit quietly in the cloister and practice reading or singing. On work days they are busy in the workshops, in copying books, in weaving clothing or doing other manual work.

"The convent is rich in religious zeal and also in income. It has no tall buildings, but all the rooms are large, beautiful and monastic. All the workshops have running water and are well equipped. The convent supports 50 nuns, also many guests, who are never lacking, and a number of servants. The mother is kind to all, gives good advice to everyone who asks for it, resolves the most difficult problems presented to her, writes books, instructs her sisters, leads sinners back to the right path and is always fully occupied."[7]

[7]Pitra, Analecta Sacra VIII, Monte Cassino 1882, 405.

# CHAPTER 5

# DECLINE AND REFORM

At the beginning of the thirteenth century, a new religious ideal was formulated with the rise of the two mendicant orders, Franciscans and Dominicans. The rapid growth of these two orders coincided with the decline of the old Benedictine monachism. During the following two centuries, Benedictinism had a very limited influence in the development of cultural and ascetic life, despite the fact that for half a millennium it had shown the way in that field and had been almost the only decisive force.

This decline of the old monastic ideal also affected the convents, which were closely affiliated with the monasteries, since they no longer received inspiration, stimulus or help of any kind from these monasteries. Their economic, religious and cultural decline was so great that many Benedictine convents scarcely deserved the name of religious institutes. This was at a time when the convents of the Poor Clares, Dominicans and many Cistercian convents portrayed the old ideal of contemplation and the mystical life in a most glorious manner, and also ranked high in cultural development. So it is understandable that women, sincere in their dedication to Christ the Lord, flocked to these convents.

There were a number of reasons for the DECLINE of Benedictinism. As already indicated, the convents were generally small manors with widely scattered possessions entrusted to vassals, tenants or serfs. The introduction of the monetary system instead of the old system of barter brought about an economic crisis. To obtain money, many convents had to mortgage their possessions, and if they could not redeem the mortgage, they lost their property. Furthermore, vassals and tenants availed themselves of hard times or the reign of a weak abbess as an opportunity to obtain possession of the convent property which they had held only in fee. Because of crop failures and general poverty the convent did not receive the necessary deliveries of farm products, and the nuns suffered want. In this way even convents that were once wealthy were forced into economic straits.

Thirteenth-century monastic history became economic history. Abbesses, who in all seriousness assumed responsibility for preserving the rights and property of the convent and providing for it, had to fight to maintain the possessions of the convent. Endless feuds now fill the annals of the convents. The imperial and prince abbeys had disputes with their subjects, and a Benedictine convent hardly had the appearance of a religious organization. The economic situation necessitated a division of community funds. There was a fund for the abbess which sustained her and her little household, and a fund for the convent, from which the nuns lived and which they themselves administered. The benefice of the abbess was generally 20 times that of a simple nun.

Since the fund for nuns was often small, it was no longer possible to receive many nuns into the convent, and their number declined more and more. The decline in numbers was connected with another evil which had an unwholesome effect, the system of accepting only women of the nobility into the convent. In the early Middle Ages religious motives prompted parents to give their children to the convent. In the thirteenth and fourteenth centuries, however, the offering of children by noble families was only a question of providing for them according to their rank. The nobility watched jealously that no one except their daughters be received into the convent so that their own children would be adequately cared for.

These children of the nobility received very little specialized religious training and grew up without any inner attraction toward the religious life. Since the old convent schools no longer existed, the life lacked spiritual foundation, and they spent their days in idleness. A sense of duty prompted them to maintain a minimum of choir service, as being proper to a religious institution, but it was considered only a traditional formality. The nuns considered it, as did the cathedral chapter and the canonesses, merely as a duty to be performed. The sublime religious sentiments once inspired by the psalmody had long since disappeared.

A third evil was the example of the canonesses. The institute of canonesses became ever more worldly and finally proved to be only an institute of secular ladies. But their manner of life became the pattern and model for many Benedictine convents, which had the ambition to become like them. In some Benedictine convents the old order of discipline slipped back so far, or the traditions were so completely lost, that they scarcely knew to which rule they actually subscribed. In fact, many Benedictine convents even took the last step and upon payment of a stipend permitted the Roman curia to change them into institutes of canonesses. This happened in France at Maubeuge, Bourbourg, Baume-les-Dames, Remiremont, in Belgium at Mons, in Alsace at Hohenburg and Othmarsheim, in Hessen at Kaufungen.

Other convents simply gave themselves a rule which corresponded completely to the observance of an institute of canonesses. An example of this was the prince abbey of Rynsburg, where the nuns were paid stipends for participation in choir service as were the cathedral canons. On feast days in this wealthy prince abbey there was musical entertainment at table by drummers, fifers and buglers. When the abbess appeared for High Mass or Vespers, or when she took part in a procession, she was preceded by her retinue: the chaplain, two or three servants and a chamberlain. If she went on a journey she added to this retinue a nun chaplain.[1]

On Palm Sunday the nuns took part in the blessing of palms in the city church, viewed the procession and returned to the convent church to complete the Office. On Mondays, Wednesdays,

[1] Translator's note: "An appointment in the nunnery which has led to some controversy is that of chaplain, it being alleged by some writers that the chaplain of the convent was necessarily a man. Certainly in most houses, especially in the wealthier ones, there were men chaplains. But the fact that the chaplain's office could be and was held by a woman is established beyond doubt by the following information. In consequence of an episcopal visitation (1478) of the Benedictine convent of Easebourne, injunctions were sent to the prioress, one of which directs that 'every week beginning with the eldest, excepting the subprioress, she shall select for herself in due course and in turns one of her nuns as chaplain (capelanissam) for divine service and to wait upon herself.' This injunction is in accordance with the words of Chaucer, who says that the prioress who was on a pilgrimage to Canterbury had with her a nun who acted as chaplain to her (line 163):
 'Another Nonne also with hire hadde sche
 That was hire chapelleine, and priestes thre.'
. . . How far the woman chaplain performed the same offices as the man chaplain seems impossible to tell; probably she recited the inferior services in the chapel of the nunnery." Lina Eckenstein, *Woman under Monasticism*, 376-377.

Fridays and Saturdays there was a common stroll beyond convent grounds. If a nun received a visit from her relatives, she could eat with them in the guest house. There was also a common meal with all visitors upon entrance of a nun into the convent. At her entrance the noble lady appeared in a garment of gold cloth and a fur-trimmed mantle. The latter was presented to the convent as a gift or could be redeemed for money by the relatives.

The consequence of all these evils was that the number of nuns in a convent in the fourteenth and fifteenth centuries was very small. The German convents had on an average only eight or ten nuns, some even less. In France and England it was not much better. There the Black Plague swept away many nuns, and the Hundred Years' War brought plunder and disturbance to many convents in France or burdened them with such taxes that they had only a wretched existence. Both in England and in France there were convents in which only one or two nuns still lived, and in France many died out completely.

As regards the monastic life, in so far as one could still speak of it, the convent property was divided into individual benefices, which were attached to the offices the nuns held in the convent. The nun lived from this benefice, and only as many nuns were received as there were benefices, so that a new reception occurred only when a benefice was freed by someone's death. Numerous noble families who wished to provide for a daughter founded such a benefice at the child's entrance into the convent. The income went to her alone during her lifetime and devolved upon the convent only at her death. In this manner individuals provided for themselves.

There was therefore private ownership, and generally there was no longer a common meal, as each one had her meals provided for her by a servant. Often no vows were pronounced, but there still remained an installation in choir as was the custom with canonesses. Obviously the enclosure had completely vanished: nuns made visits to the city or to their relatives; on feast days many guests were entertained in the convent; nuns went to weddings and even to dances. The clothing was very worldly: nuns wore furs, fine lace veils which permitted the hair to show through, pointed shoes, rings and earrings. Frequently the only thing that remained of the convent was the old name.

About the middle of the thirteenth century the Roman curia applied drastic measures to the convents of Italy, where the decline in discipline was the same. It ceded the great abbeys which had lost their property and their means of support as commenda to cardinals or prelates or disbanded them completely and gave them to the Poor Clares or Dominicans on the assumption that no reform in the Benedictine order could be expected from within.

In the spirit of historical truth and justice it must be said that very few convents came to actual moral corruption. Deplorable as the above-mentioned improprieties were from the standpoint of the ideal of monastic life—private ownership, abolition of the enclosure, worldly clothing, etc.—they were after all in keeping with the regular order of the institute of canonesses. Very few nuns considered the situation unseemly, since they found it at their entrance, and many may have lived a personally pious life. It was not simply insubordination, and hardly ever do we hear anything of actual scandal.

Of course there was no advanced religious life in such convents. It was the task of the abbesses to rule their little territory well, to preserve the possessions of the convent through all oppression and crisis, and to keep the convent buildings and the church in repair. The abbesses deserve credit for doing these things, even though their first duty should have been to preserve the religious life. This duty, however, they could not do alone; they needed the help of monks and priests, and they found very little support from those quarters in the time of Avignon and the great Western schism.

The decline had reached its lowest point about the beginning of the fifteenth century, and it was just at this time that salvation came to the convents in their extremity. The renewal of the religious life started in ITALY. The monasteries led the way. After their own regeneration, they again recognized their great duty to their sisters, who had also been the glory of Benedictinism for so many centuries.

The monastic revival took its origin from the monastery of St. Justina in Padua, whose restorer was the noble Louis Barbo († 1443). He was responsible not only for the restoration of this old abbey but also for the founding of a new Benedictine congregation, which goes down in Benedictine history as the Cassinese

Congregation. The monks of the young congregation also assumed the responsibility for the convents, and a number of city convents, such as those of Brescia, Vicenza, Milan, Ferrara and Cremona, became associated with the union of St. Justina.

They received the same constitution and observance as the congregation. The lifelong rule of abbesses was abolished: there were only prioresses with three-year terms. They were installed at the general chapter and remained under the direction of the president of the congregation or of the general chapter in all things. This form of Benedictine life, very far removed from the earlier traditions, found great acceptance in the Romance countries and spread quickly, thanks to the support of the Roman curia.

The renewal of the monastic life in the GERMAN CONVENTS followed a little later. The first beginnings were made in southern Germany and coincided with the strengthening of the Benedictine ideal associated with the names of the monasteries of Melk in Austria and Kastel in the upper Palatinate. Both monasteries produced a new observance based on the customs of Hirsau. Since this observance was used in many monasteries of southern Germany, it also exercised a good influence on many convents and brought forth new life after years and decades of decline.

The noble and influential Cardinal NICHOLAS OF CUSA († 1464) proved himself a special friend of Benedictine monachism at this time of early reform, which received its impetus from the councils of Constance and Basle. He held the opinion that a reform in the Church was possible only if preceded by a monastic reform and only if the renewal of the life in the Church had its center in good monasteries. In the year 1452 the Cardinal, in his capacity of apostolic legate and visitator for Germany, issued decrees which were binding for the religious houses of both monks and nuns: residence outside the monastery was forbidden, whether in city dwellings or on the monastery farms; the resumption of the monastic life was regulated by the abolition of private ownership and a stricter enclosure. The principal evils of conventual life were thereby removed, provided the laws of the Cardinal were obeyed.

The kind of opposition the Cardinal encountered, however, is shown in the conflict that arose with the convent of Sonnenburg in his diocese of Brixen when he tried to get his regulations recognized and accepted. The discipline of the convent had deteriorated completely, so that the nuns no longer lived a monastic life in any way. They took part in weddings, plays, dances, visited health resorts, and each one managed her own property. When the Cardinal interfered and entrusted the visitation of the convent to Lawrence of Ahausen, the nuns protested against it and turned to Duke Sigismund of Austria. At first they subscribed to the statutes of reform but soon recanted and opposed every attempt to introduce the new order into their convent. The Cardinal therefore deposed and excommunicated Abbess Verena, and appointed Afra of Velseck as abbess; but she had no success. Since the nuns found an advocate in Duke Sigismund, the inner conventual strife became a political conflict which involved not only the chanceries of Vienna and Brixen but also over a period of years the Roman curia, and threw the whole country into an uproar.

The noble-convent of Urspring in Württemberg furnished another example of this kind. Inspired by praiseworthy zeal, the mistress Margaret of Freiburg went to the convent of Heggbach one day to acquaint herself with the new reform. She was then going to introduce it into her own convent. She found understanding and also agreement from the abbot of St. George in the Black Forest, spiritual superior of the convent, as well as from some of the nuns. She received effective assistance from Duchess Mechtild, who had her widow's estate at Rottenburg and was descended from the family of the overseer of Margaret's own convent of Urspring. Mechtild had interested several of the nuns of the already reformed convent of St. Walburg in transmitting the new manner of life to Urspring.

She herself wanted to introduce these nuns into Urspring, and one day she appeared with them at the convent entrance together with some abbots, several preaching friars and a number of noblemen to assist her in case she met opposition from the nuns. Some noblemen of the opposite party also appeared. Under the direction of Barbara von Stein, the group of obstinate nuns who refused the reform had withdrawn into the isolated infirmary in the convent garden and there fortified themselves by barricading the doors with tables, benches, blocks of wood and stones. They themselves occupied the upper floor and appeared at the windows, showing their weapons: stones, sticks, whips and spears. The duchess gave her people the command to attack the house. But the noblemen objected, explaining that it would always remain a disgrace if they fought against women. Besides, they did not wish to make enemies with their equals; after all, these were noblewomen, and nuns too.

The duchess then had the alarm sounded from the nearby bell tower. This brought the common people. The simple townsmen and peasants were prepared to attack and they stormed the house. Those nuns who resisted were bound and put under arrest. Only after this could the nuns from St. Walburg make an entrance. The nuns who did not wish to accept the reform could go to other convents or to relatives. A good many of them returned contrite to Urspring after a long time, and Barbara von Stein herself submitted to the new order. Since the abbess acted with great discretion and prudence, peace and quiet were gradually restored to the convent, and Urspring became a model of regular observance.[2]

In the Rhineland Abbot JOHN RODE († 1439) of St. Matthias in Trier was the one who reawakened interest in the monastic life. Through his efforts the noble-convent Marienberg at Boppard was brought to a new flowering. He himself visited the convent and found in Abbess Isengard von Greiffenklau († 1469) complete understanding of the desire for reform. Isengard was a distinguished woman, and the convent chronicle says of her: "Like the sun among the stars, so she towered above the nuns by her gifts of nature and her charm."

John Rode prepared statutes for Marienberg, which later found their way into a number of other convents. These statutes came to St. Irmina's in Trier, Oberwerth at Coblenz and St. Walburg's in Eichstätt. The reputation of Marienberg, which now as before was a convent for nobility, rose so that under Isengard's successor, her niece Christine von Greiffenklau, the number of nuns reached 150, and among them were the two daughters, Johanna and Anna, of Count Louis of the Rhenish Palatinate.

Even more important than the revival in southern Germany and in the Rhineland was that in northern Germany, which started from the abbey of BURSFELD. In its beginnings it was very closely associated with the work of Abbot John Rode. Bishops,

[2]Stud. u. Mitt. OSB 38, 1917, 232 f.

abbots and rulers, zealous for reform, gladly led the convents under their jurisdiction to the Bursfeld reform. For the reform gave the convents not only a new manner of life but also, by uniting them in the strong bond of the congregation, a guarantee of security.

The change was not easily made in all convents. In some, especially in the convents of the nobility, the nuns called upon their relatives to help preserve the old manner of life. In other instances, after the reform two convents lived side by side: the unreformed, preserving its traditions, and the reformed, following the new order.

This solution to the conflict between the old and the new had the general approval of the abbots of the Bursfeld union, and no one of the old observance was forced to accept the new manner of life. Yet they must promise not to disturb the new order and were barred from official positions in the convent. If the abbess did not wish to accept the new observance she must resign. The new abbess, who very often came from a convent already reformed, generally brought some nuns from such a convent, who assisted her and introduced the new spirit to the young members of the house.

The success of the Bursfeld Congregation was very significant. About the year 1500 there were approximately 66 convents in which the Bursfeld influence showed its effect, but not all the convents actually belonged to the union. There were 31 directly connected with it, among them Marienberg at Boppard, Oberwerth at Coblenz, Niederprüm, Burtscheid at Aachen, Rolandswerth, Neuwerk at M.-Gladbach, Willebadessen, St. Mauritius, St. Agatha and the convent of the Machabees in Cologne, as well as a number of important prince abbeys of distinction, which preserved their old rank but had the obligation of accepting candidates not of the nobility. Other convents accepted only the observance of the Bursfeld union and formed a confraternity with it. They also received a confessor from a Bursfeld abbey, but remained under the jurisdiction of the diocesan bishop, who, however, frequently yielded his visitation rights to an abbot of the Bursfeld union.

The statutes for the convents were modeled on those of the monasteries.[3] Regarding the reception of new members it was

[3]Johannes Linneborn, *Der Zustand der westfälischen Benediktinerklöster in den*

ordered that no one under 12 years of age could be received as
a novice. If children were brought as oblates, this oblation was
binding only with the free decision of the child as she reached
maturity. Profession was generally made at the age of 16. As a
matter of principle any virgin should be able to enter; the limita-
tion to the nobility was abolished.

Novices were instructed in various school subjects and must
above all learn the Latin language. The nuns among themselves
and especially in conversation with priests and monks should
use only Latin. The vow of stability was made to the convent in
which one entered, and yet every novice must promise to allow
herself to be sent to another convent in the interests of the reform. Every convent was to have a school for the education of the
monastic recruits, and if the convent itself had no capable teachers
they must be obtained from the outside.

The abbess was elected for life by the members of the convent
under the supervision of the visitator. Under oath she had to
promise at her installation to preserve the Bursfeld observance
and support the decrees of the general chapter. A visitation was
held every three years, and the visitator with the consent of the
president of the congregation could deprive the abbess of her
office if she had worked against these decrees or if it was established that she was unfit to perform the duties of her office.

Besides choir service, the occupation of the nuns was the performance of domestic work in kitchen, house and garden. In addition every nun should be able to do some kind of hand work:
sewing, weaving, embroidery, bookbinding, preparing parch-
ment and the like. Copying and illuminating manuscripts was
highly recommended. It was considered the noblest task, for the
statutes declare that "it is nearest to the spiritual." Indeed great
things were accomplished in this sphere, and the calligraphy of
the Middle Ages was revived.

The canonical Hours were sung completely every day and current popular devotions were added. There were weekly confes-

50 Jahren vor ihrem Anschluss an die Bursfelder Kongregation, Münster in West-
phalia 1898.
—Die Reformation der westfälischen Benediktinerklöster im 15. Jahrhundert
durch die Bursfelder Kongregation, Stud. u. Mitt. OSB 20, 1899, 1-190.
—Die Bursfelder Kongregation während der ersten 100 Jahre ihres Bestehens,
Deutsche Geschichtsblätter 1912, 3-58.

An enumeration of the Bursfeld convents is given by Ph. Hofmeister, Liste der
Nonnenklöster der Bursfelder Kongregation, Stud. u. Mitt. OSB 53, 1935, 77-102.

sions and monthly reception of Holy Communion. Some of their hygienic practices show how sound their asceticism was: during the summer a bath was taken every six weeks, in winter every eight weeks, but the bath was permitted to the sick and feeble more frequently. The hair was to be washed every two weeks.

The enclosure was strictly kept. The door to the enclosure of the nuns had two locks;[4] the provost had the key to the one and the abbess to the other, and the door could be opened only with the cooperation of both, as one lock was on the outside of the door and the other on the inside. Visits in the parlor were made only through a grill. Yet the enclosure did not mean a complete locking up. The abbess could travel to pay homage or to attend the general chapter, and the nuns were likewise permitted to take trips in the interests of the congregation.

There were three classes of members in the convent. The first group—and they were in the majority—were the nuns. The second group were the lay sisters, who did the house work. They did not take part in choir service, praying only a *Pater Noster* office instead, but they did make the vows. The third group were the *donates,* who made no vows but only a promise of obedience to the abbess. Since they were not bound by the enclosure, they did the errands and wore a gray dress in contrast to the black habit of the Benedictine nun.

A beneficial expansion of the convents took place under the Bursfeld abbots and monks. No attempt was made to set up a new monastic ideal in the Bursfeld union. The reformers were content to remove the principal evils from which the convents suffered: private ownership, living separately, and neglecting the enclosure. They did not care for observance of the Rule according to the letter, but wanted a good observance according to the spirit. What they considered essential was poverty, communal life and choir service, united with simple piety and solid ascetic effort without excess or singularity. The old organization of the convents was also preserved, permitting every convent a certain independence and yet supporting it firmly through the union, the abbot visitor and the general chapter. Certain house traditions were prudently tolerated along with the general Bursfeld observance, provided they did not go against the general order.

[4]Translator's note: See Valentine Theodore Schaaf, O.F.M., *The Cloister,* Cincinnati 1921, 29, 106, 131.

A noble intellectual life flowered again in the convents, and the joy of study was reawakened in the spirit of classical learning. The DEVOTIO MODERNA with its simplicity, its discretion and quiet composure found a home in Benedictine convents, and intellectual work thrived again in this gentle atmosphere. As in Anglo-Saxon times and also in the Middle Ages the nuns now again had contact with scholars, exchanging letters with them. Many famous humanists, like Abbot John Trithemius († 1516) and the prior of Maria Laach, John Butzbach († 1516), found pleasure in corresponding with learned cloistered nuns, and more than one left a literary monument to them. John Butzbach, for instance, impressed by the new learning in the convents, wrote a book about scholarly nuns. He considered the highly educated Aleidis of Rolandswerth the ideal of a learned nun.

As in Germany so in the old monastic country of FRANCE the religious life in the convents blossomed forth anew; here too only ruin remained after the catastrophes which had befallen France since the middle of the fourteenth century. The reform ideas emanating from Constance and Basle bore fruit here also. The renewal began in the convent of St. Paul at Beauvais in 1468. From here new light and new strength radiated into many convents.

At the same time the religious life was strengthened in the order of Fontevrault, and from there a powerful stream flowed to the old Benedictine abbeys. The famous old abbey of Chelles was among the first affected by the movement, and from Chelles the revival spread to the old abbeys of Montmartre, Jouarre, Faremoutiers, St. Peter in Rheims and Val de Grâce. Some of these abbeys reformed from Chelles formed a union with the abbess of Chelles as leader and the Benedictine monks as spiritual directors.

Foremost among the noble bishops zealous for reform by resuming care of the convents was the archbishop of Paris, Stephen Pancher († 1519), who issued statutes for the convents under his jurisdiction. These statutes received great acclaim and were introduced into many convents.

Cardinal Amboise showed an equally zealous concern for the affairs of the convents. His sister Magdalena was abbess in Saint-Menoux, and his niece Marie of Rochechouard was abbess in Charenton. In 1503 the Cardinal brought these convents to a new regular observance, which also spread to other convents. To assure the success of the reform the Cardinal had these convents unite with the Benedictine congregation of Chezal-Benoît, which at that time had begun as a reformed congregation in France and enjoyed an excellent reputation. Later, this congregation joined that of St. Maur. When the Maurists refused to accept convents of women into their union, the convents were again placed under the bishops. The convent of Nevers joined the congregation of Cluny.

In SPAIN the majority of convents joined the congregation of the Claustrales—San Daniel of Gerona, San Pedro de las Puellas, which enjoyed greater privileges, Santa Cruz de las Sorores. They followed the constitutions drawn up for the monks of the congregation. Other Benedictine convents joined the reform congregation of Valladolid, which like that of Chezal-Benoît followed the principles of the congregation of St. Justina and therefore was centrally directed by a superior general, who had full authority over the individual convents. El Moral, Oviedo and Santa Cruz de Sahagun belonged to this congregation. Each convent had only a prioress or an abbess whose term of office was restricted. In 1583 this system was approved by Pope Gregory XIII and prescribed for all the convents of Italy and adjoining islands. The superior could be elected or appointed for a period of three years only, but after this term a re-election or reappointment was possible.

The splendid development of the convents at the beginning of the sixteenth century was very seriously affected by the outbreak of the PROTESTANT REVOLUTION. Naturally the convents in Germany were hit very hard from the first. The Peasants' War led to the plundering of many convents, and complete destruction for some. Those of southern and middle Germany suffered particularly heavy losses. In Thuringia plundering was the fate of Allendorf, Boneroda, Gerbstedt, Gerode, Helfta, Holzzelle and Walbeck, and in the land of Fulda it befell Zelle and Thulba.

In the districts that went over to Lutheranism the very existence of the convents was at stake. The ruling princes generally did not use brutal force but for the most part permitted the convents to die out gradually, since reception of novices was forbidden. Their property was confiscated and so further existence was impossible. As domains of the state, the property of the former convents was incorporated into landed property of the state, and several, especially in northern Germany, became Protestant foundations for nobility.

An attempt was often made also to lead the nuns into the Lutheran faith, with success in only a few cases. For the most part the confiscation of property and the closing of convents followed only upon the death of the last abbess or the last nun, so great was the resistance in general.

There were touching examples of faithfulness and perseverance in vocation. In Ebstorf in the year 1533 the nuns declared to their ruler, upon his repeated exhortations to embrace the new teaching, that there was no reason for them to turn from the old Church, that they must not do so for the sake of their souls, and that he might spare himself the trouble of sending them preachers or taking any other such measures. In Walrode the closing of the convent occurred in 1538 when Abbess Anne Behr, because of her advanced age, could not perform her official duties. A Lutheran nun took her place.

The convent of Lüne offered heroic opposition. It had made great progress since the acceptance of the reform in 1481. Thirty-six novices made their profession on one day in 1486, and in 1526 the convent had 87 choir nuns, so that it was one of the largest convents. The duke ordered the nuns to listen to the sermons of an apostate Dominican. When he said in a sermon that there were only two sacraments, Abbess Mathilde Willen left with all her nuns.

To expel the preacher from the church they resorted to a unique method. They burned old furs and rags in the sacristy, and the chronicle relates "that there was such a stench in the church that the preacher together with all the people was forced to leave." Only in 1562, after the death of the last Catholic nun, was the convent confiscated.

As a result of the Protestant Revolution 76 abbeys and 7 priories of Benedictine nuns were destroyed in Germany, as well as 137 abbeys of Cistercian nuns.

The Revolution also brought the decline of all Benedictine convents in Denmark, Norway, Sweden, Iceland, as well as some in Holland and Switzerland.

The fate of the ENGLISH CONVENTS was also sad. About 1500, there were still 84 Benedictine convents in England with 850 nuns. Most of the houses were small priories; only 12 were considered wealthy convents.

A monastic record of 1534 gives us a glimpse into the life of the English Benedictine nuns of that time. They had lived the monastic life on an eminently high plane, despite the various hardships which had come upon the convents during the course of the fifteenth century. The doors of the convents were locked in the evening after Compline and were opened again in the morning at 6 o'clock in summer, 7 o'clock in winter. Likewise the dormitories remained locked until the beginning of divine service. In the choir, cloister, refectory and dormitory silence reigned.

Without permission from the abbess or prioress no nun could leave the convent. Permission to leave the house was given if the journey was of benefit to the convent, and also to visit parents or relatives. The period of time away from the convent as set down by the superior could not be exceeded. The nuns should always be accompanied on a journey by a sister. Once a year the accounts must be open for inspection. The noon meal was at 11 o'clock and that in the evening at 5 o'clock. All received the same food, which was served them by maids. A fire should be kept in the refectory from All Saints until Good Friday.

Many convents also had an extern school in which young girls were instructed in cooking, baking, sewing, nursing, reading, writing and painting.

The suppression of the convents resulted from force almost everywhere, since the nuns generally refused to surrender their convents to the king voluntarily. In 1539, the work of closing the convents was ended. After an existence of almost 900 years there no longer remained a single convent in England.

Thus the Protestant Revolution had seriously disturbed the new development of monastic life and in many lands destroyed it completely.

# CHAPTER 6

## REVIVAL OF CONVENTS AND
## CONGREGATIONS IN THE PERIOD OF THE
## CATHOLIC RESTORATION

Under the influence of the reform ideas which originated at the Council of Trent, monastic life blossomed forth again in the Benedictine convents of the different countries. The revival was reminiscent of the great times of the past.

Catholic FRANCE was foremost among all countries: it rose to the first place in European culture, and in the sphere of piety also it assumed the leadership of Christendom. Again it became a land of convents.

After the first reforms at the beginning of the sixteenth century, of which mention has already been made and which in spite of undoubted success affected only individual convents, there followed religious wars which brought France to the brink of the abyss. The monastic life was seriously retarded. Many convents were plundered, some devastated, and, for the most part, regular life was scarcely possible.

In most of the convents there remained only a few nuns who, in great need, arranged their life as well as they could. Other convents became worldly and the nuns differed very little in their dress from ladies in the world. It is reported that whenever the nuns of the convent La Déserte in Lyons chose to do so, they appeared in the church in secular dress and sang the Office without being separated from the people. This convent would soon play a great role in the reform.

But now began a restoration which affected almost all the old convents of France, led to many new foundations and to the formation of two new Benedictine congregations which were filled with great ascetic zeal. A glorious monastic spring flourished and

61

yielded the richest fruit.[1] The restoration resulted from a large number of outstanding abbesses, truly great personalities, who were filled with heroism and enthusiasm, and who through the charm of their personalities, the nobility of their hearts and the grand scale of their activities, won large numbers of high-minded girls for St. Benedict and his convents.

The aim in this revival of conventual life was not simply the restoration of regular discipline through a literal observance of the Rule of St. Benedict; it was much more the formation of a living piety from the spirit of the Catholic Restoration. The new ideals of the times gave these convents their character. The Rule of St. Benedict was only the foundation on which the new edifice could be erected. Different kinds of austerities were introduced, especially penitential practices, in conformity with the spirit of the times and also with the wholesome judgment of the abbesses.

The abbesses and the newly formed congregations were guided by the great spiritual teachers of this period such as St. Francis de Sales, Bérulle, and the orders which had the leadership in the Counter-Reformation and the Catholic Restoration: Jesuits, Capuchins and Oratorians, now joined by the Benedictines. The Council of Trent had pointed the direction for the reform. Its principal demands were: introduction of the strict enclosure with complete seclusion from the world, careful selection in the reception of novices, observance of the year of probation, profession only at maturity, and ascetic life in accordance with such practices of piety as were common at that time.

In general the restoration encountered no great opposition. The women were soon caught up in the current of the religious movement. Often enough their old life no longer pleased the residents of the convents. They willingly relinquished their places to the young, who introduced a new ideal; often, in fact, they even joined them.

To be sure, there were also isolated cases of opposition. A report from Pommeraie indicates that two resisting nuns declared they would jump from the convent walls if the new order were introduced. They sent out letters full of hostility and complaints against the abbess. In La Déserte one nun started a fire, to burn the abbess in her room. These were the exceptions. The diffi-

<hr>

[1]H. Brémond, *Histoire littéraire du sentiment religieux en France* II, Paris 1923, ch. 6, "Les grandes abbesses," 394-536.

culties were not generally the introduction of the enclosure but the restoration of the communal life or even more frequently the change of habit, since the nuns did not wish to relinquish the white clothing or the lace veil.

There were also touching examples of sisterly love in those convents in which the reform was to be introduced. This was true in Flines. Here Florence de Werquignoeul wanted to introduce the reform, but the older nuns could not be influenced to give up their accustomed manner of life. Florence, therefore, decided to leave with the younger ones. She settled with them near Douai, where she founded the convent of Our Lady of Peace. The leave-taking from Flines was a tearful one, and all those remaining assured those who left that they could return at any time if the life in the new convent should prove too hard.

A leading place, if not the first place, in the work of renewal was occupied by the time-honored abbey of MONTMARTRE in Paris. The one who revived the religious life here was the great Abbess Marie de Beauvillier († 1657). During her term of office she gave the veil to 227 nuns and sent more than 50 into other houses to reform or make new foundations. Her spiritual director and guide was the Capuchin Benedict of Canfeld.

Among those who received their intellectual and religious formation at Montmartre was Margaretha d'Arbouze († 1626), who became abbess of Val de Grâce. The constitutions which she issued for her convent with the advice of the general visitator of the Feuillants, Eustache Asseline, were introduced into many other convents. Abbesses as well as nuns came to Val de Grâce to learn the life there and thus pattern the observance in their own convent on it. The convent was highly regarded by the French court. Anne of Austria, wife of King Louis XIII, decreed that the hearts of all deceased princes and princesses of the royal house of France should be kept in the convent church of Val de Grâce. This was done until 1789.

Finally, mention must be made of La Déserte in Lyons, which rose to a place of prominence under the direction of Abbess Margaretha de Quibly, a disciple and close friend of St. Francis de Sales. She also drew up statutes for her abbey which were adopted in other places.

In 1604 Florence de Werquignoeul, already mentioned, founded the reformed convent at Douai, which became the starting point for other reformed convents in France. In Arras, Namur, Liège, Mons and other convents this manner of life was introduced. These convents were noted for the fact that they were dedicated to the education of girls and admitted young girls into their houses for intellectual and cultural training.

The revival of the religious life also brought the convents to a renewal of intellectual activity. The abbesses were generally persons of high intellectual attainment. They were in close contact with the leaders of the new Christian humanism, and correspondence as well as personal meetings with these men led to the finest results in the intellectual sphere. Reading was zealously fostered, and books were again written in many convents.

It is regrettable that the Benedictine monks took so little part in this revival of the regular life in the Benedictine convents, and left this work to the newer orders. The two great reform congregations of St. Vanne and St. Maur had great scholarly aims and believed that through the spiritual direction of nuns they would lose valuable strength which they needed for the work of the congregation. The Maurist congregation refused on principle to take convents into their union, making an exception only for the famous abbey of Chelles.

The result was that the convents received a formation which in many ways was far removed from the old Benedictine traditions. The young pupils, spiritually eager, took up with enthusiasm what their teachers in the spiritual life offered. These teachers naturally acquainted them with the new ascetical writings, having no Benedictine tradition themselves and no foundation that would enable them to start out from the early medieval spirituality.

Among the nuns there were women gifted with intellect and discrimination, who recognized and deplored this. Jacqueline de Blemur († 1696), who entered the convent of the Holy Trinity at Caen, where she acted as prioress and novice mistress before she joined Catherine de Bar, foundress of the Association of Perpetual Adoration, said about this, "The Benedictines have the intrinsic right above all other orders to transmit to us the spirit of the order of St. Benedict. No one can give what he himself does not have; religious of other orders can awaken in the soul the dispositions for virtue in general but not in particular for the virtues of St. Benedict, whose principles are not their study."

Jacqueline was a woman of high culture and left a number of writings which portray broad knowledge as well as an excellent spiritual schooling. Her lives of Benedictine saints in seven volumes, *L'Année Bénédictine,* was widely read and translated into many languages. Of greater importance, however, was her work *Eloges de Personnes Illustres en Piété de l'Ordre de S. Benoît en ces Derniers Siècles,* actually a history of the reforms and the piety of her time. The celebrated Benedictine scholar, Jean Mabillon, after her death wrote the obituary that was sent to all the convents.

The nuns in the abbeys of this new reform kept the traditions in so far as they performed their choir service, and also observed with great zeal the practices of piety peculiar to the new orders. There is no doubt that by these means their spiritual life was intensified. In Cluny there had been great emphasis on reforming the exterior life of the community through the ceremonial and the celebration of the solemn choir services. Now the emphasis was shifted to self-perfection. Meditation was considered most important and was to accompany choir prayer itself. It was quite universally recommended that meditation on the Passion of Christ accompany recitation of the Office regardless of the text of the psalm.

The above-mentioned Jacqueline de Blemur related how the new methods of meditation were introduced at Caen. As she says, no one there knew this form of prayer. Abbess Laurentia de Budos heard of it, and every evening, after the rest of the nuns had retired, she went into the church with her secretary and there practiced meditative prayer according to the new method. After she had done this for a year and was quite experienced in it, she asked a Jesuit priest to give her nuns instructions on it. Then a ten-day retreat was held and meditation introduced. At first the younger nuns knelt near the abbess and received whispered aspirations from their spiritual mother when their own thoughts ran out.

Thus the great concern of the reform convents was not simply the removal of abuses, nor the introduction of a stricter life in the spirit of the Rule or the traditions of the Middle Ages; the first concern was the interior life, the life of union with God— in fact, the mystical life. And so mystics of high rank came from these convents: Marie Alocquin, Margaretha d'Arbouze, Charlotte Le Sergent, Marie Granger, abbess of Montargis, and Jeanne Delaloc, prioress of Poperinghe.

Asceticism and mysticism were linked together in these convents. The French Benedictine nuns allowed themselves to be inundated by the mystic stream whose source arose in the Spanish Carmel. Many of them were in close relationship and friendship with Carmelite nuns, and their zeal for austerities was hardly less than that of the Carmelites.

A touch of greatness cannot be denied them, and it is significant for these convents that they exercised so great an attraction for the women of nobility. As one goes through the names of abbesses or nuns, one finds the most illustrious names of old France, which were to be destroyed in the bloodthirsty Revolution: Bourbon, Bar, Lothringen, Guise, Orléans, Oranien, Béthune, Choiseul, Foix, to name only a few. Among them were princesses of royal blood, related with the ruling houses of Austria, Spain, England and Scotland. They also deserve credit for the fact that the convents everywhere were places of highest culture and, despite the strict enclosure, remained vitally united with the high culture of Catholic France. The time from 1590 to 1700 could be considered a golden period in the history of Benedictine nuns.

The revival of the religious spirit was not restricted to the old Benedictine abbeys, many of which stemmed from the eighth century; it also led to the foundation of two new Benedictine congregations, both of which were destined to be very influential. There is no denying that they retreated still further from Benedictine tradition than did the recognized old convents. The Rule of St. Benedict was for them scarcely more than a form, as the Rule of St. Augustine or of St. Francis was for other new foundations of this and later times, since the Roman curia required of all new congregations the acceptance of an older rule. The contemplative orders adopted the Rule of St. Benedict, but their religious life was formed by the particular devotions and piety which attracted them and inspired their foundation, and also by their constitutions, drawn up according to the spirit of the times. Two devotions performed in the spirit of reparation and penance were responsible for these new Benedictine foundations: meditation on the Passion of Christ and adoration of the Blessed Sacrament of the altar.

The first of these congregations was the Benedictine nuns of

CALVARY.[2] The foundress of the community was ANTOINETTE D'ORLÉANS-LONGUEVILLE (†1618). She was at first a Feuillantine, that is, a Cistercian of a special observance in Toulouse. In 1605 she was named coadjutor to the abbess of Fontevrault by Pope Paul V, but she left this abbey in 1611 to lead a stricter life. The famous Capuchin, Father Joseph de Temple, trusted co-worker of Cardinal Richelieu and known as "his Gray Eminence," became her spiritual adviser. At first she lived in the convent L'Encloître in the diocese of Poitiers, which she brought to such a flourishing condition that within six years she received 100 novices.

Then with the help of Father Joseph, Antoinette founded the first convent of a new observance, the convent of Calvary at Poitiers in 1617, which was soon followed by others. Every convent was to be a Calvary, in which the memory of the sufferings of the Lord should be kept alive through zealous and constant meditation on the Passion of Christ and through participation in the Passion in the form of penances and chastisements undertaken voluntarily.

The congregation spread rapidly throughout France. Three prelates directed it and named as their representative a visitator general; they also appointed the superior general. Together the convents formed a centrally governed congregation with chapter that met every three years, although every convent was autonomous under a prioress elected by the members.

The community of Benedictine nuns of the BLESSED SACRAMENT and Perpetual Adoration had even greater influence and wider expansion than the Congregation of Calvary. Its foundress was CATHERINE DE BAR or, as she was later called, Mechtild of the Most Blessed Sacrament. She was professed in 1633 in the Annunciation convent at Bruyères, not far from her home, St. Dié. When this community had to flee before the war hordes in 1635, she found an asylum with the Benedictine nuns of Rambervillers.

Here Catherine became acquainted with the Benedictine life and changed over to this order, making her profession in 1640. But these nuns also had to flee from the turbulence of war. Catherine first found refuge at St. Mihiel and later at Montmartre in Paris. She did not remain at Montmartre, however, but in a small

[2]Ph. Hofmeister, *Die Verfassung der Kongregation der Benediktinerinnen vom Kalvarienberg*, Stud. u. Mitt. OSB 50, 1932, 249-277.

house in the suburb of St. Germain in Paris began to live the life that corresponded to her ideals.

More than once at the plundering of the various churches and convents which she experienced, she had seen how the soldiers tore open the tabernacles, desecrated the sacred hosts and performed the worst outrages on them. This had shaken her soul to the depths, and now she saw it as her task to atone for these sacrileges through special and even constant adoration of the Blessed Sacrament and through penitential practices. She won other pious virgins to this ideal and received assistance from Queen Anne of Austria, so that on March 25, 1653, the first exposition of the Blessed Sacrament took place. Anne of Austria was so devoted to this work that she herself kept an adoration hour with a candle in her hand in the little convent chapel.

The new community of adorers received its first recognition in 1661 from Pope Alexander VII, and in 1668 the cardinal of Vendôme approved the constitutions which Mechtild had drawn up with the advice of the prior of the abbey St. Germain des Prés, Ignatius Philibert. In 1676 Pope Innocent XI approved the congregation and placed it directly under the Apostolic See. Pope Innocent XII, however, abolished the exemption in 1694 and placed the convents under the supervision of the diocesan bishops.

All convents were independent, but not as abbeys, since out of humility Mechtild did not wish to bear the name and title of abbess and designated the Blessed Virgin as the true abbess for all convents. A prioress, elected every three years, was to be at the head of each house. These adoration convents spread everywhere, so that later they were more numerous in many countries than the convents of the old observance. The idea of adoration and reparation proved very fruitful everywhere and had a great attraction for religious-minded women. The first convent of Perpetual Adoration outside of France was founded in Warsaw in 1687.

In GERMANY the development of monastic life was seriously impeded by the Protestant Revolution and its consequent inner disorders. The Thirty Years' War brought unspeakable hardships to many convents, from which some were a long time recovering, while many were plundered and some completely destroyed, as for example the convent of St. Hildegard on Rupertsberg. The nuns from St. Mary at Fulda had to flee no less than five times because of the war, and three times experienced the pillage of their house.

First of all, the Council of Trent brought an inner renewal to the German convents as it had to the French. Since it required no attachment to a congregation for the convents as it did for the monasteries, their reform involved only the visitation and the formulation of statutes. Both of these were done by the bishops or abbots under whom the convents were placed. The great promoter for the reform of the convents in Germany in the spirit of Trent was the papal visitator, FELICIAN NINGUARDA († 1595). In this function he played the same role as Cardinal Nicholas of Cusa had played a century earlier, and took the Cardinal's reform statutes as a model in many ways.[3]

Ninguarda completed a visitation of the Bavarian Benedictine convents. The visitation showed no great abuses in the convents, but the observance was very mild in most of them and likened them in many respects to institutes for ladies.

A great display was made at profession, which was held completely in the style of a wedding. Banquets were given in the convent for outstanding visitors, the nuns could visit with their guests in the convent gardens and they themselves could leave the enclosure. In the afternoons and evenings they amused themselves with games. They gave plays and had much music; on Shrove Tuesday they masqueraded in harmless fashion.

The abbess lived outside the enclosure, took part in choir service only on great feast days, and for her meals, usually the evening meal, she invited several nuns, who were then excused from taking part in the night Office. A number of nuns kept a bird, a cat or a little dog in their cells. One or another might even take her lap dog to choir, where it would rest on a cushion at the feet of its mistress during choir service.

These were not great abuses, but they could not be reconciled with the seriousness of the monastic life and were not at all in keeping with the ascetical requirements and ideals of the reforms of Trent.

The result of the visitation was the issuance of statutes which regulated the conventual life in the spirit of the older traditions

[3]St. Kainz, *Nachtridentinische Reformstatuten in den deutschen Frauenklöstern des Benediktinerordens*, Stud. u. Mitt. OSB 56, 1938, 219-274.

and the new ideals of the order. The most important of these statutes were those given to the convent at Kühbach in the diocese of Augsburg in 1590, which were transmitted from there to Hohenwart and Holzen. In 1630 they came to St. Mary's in Fulda, which was settled from Kühbach. Similar statutes were given to Geisenfeld in 1589, to Nonnberg and from there to Chiemsee in 1626, also to St. Walburg's in Eichstätt in 1644 and to Niedernburg in Passau in 1670.

These statutes required no particular austerities nor did they mean a new formulation of the Benedictine ideal as was tried in the French convents. They attempted only to remove certain improprieties and to secure a good regular life. In keeping with the old Benedictine tradition they ordinarily started with the concern for the Office.

Thus the statutes of Kühbach begin: "First the religious service to which, according to the teaching of our holy father St. Benedict, nothing is to be preferred, is to be performed devoutly in choir and elsewhere, with propriety, with complete words, with long pauses, with distinct syllables, with uniform voice, not one high, another low, in singing, reading and chanting."

Concerning this, one reads in the statutes of Niedernburg: "From the teaching of the holy father Benedict it is to be noted that the prayer or psalmody shall be alert and joyful yet slow with restraint and propriety, not done lazily, not dragged and sleepily, not with yawning or half a voice, nor with swallowing or completely muffled words, but distinctly as is due the words of the Holy Spirit. While praying or singing no one should look anywhere else than toward the floor or at the book.

"One should especially avoid as much as possible speaking, laughing, playing with the hands, rumbling, rattling and coughing, also walking in and out, under heavy penance. If anyone for a very necessary reason must leave the chanting, it must be done very quietly and with proper reverence toward the crucifix and the presiding superior." Ordinarily the chanting was done standing, but sitting was permitted "because of feminine weakness."

The Office was generally led by a hebdomadarian who performed the service throughout the week. In Nonnberg there were 25 feasts of the abbess at which she presided at the Office and 29 of the prioress. The abbess had all first class feasts, also the four great feasts of the Blessed Virgin, the feasts of St. Benedict and

St. Michael. In general the Office was recited, but daily Vespers, the High Mass and the Hour before the High Mass were sung. On feasts of the abbess, Vespers were sung *figuraliter,* and the choir director provided for the musical instruments.

Until the beginning of the Thirty Years' War, Matins was said ordinarily at midnight, after which the nuns again retired until about 5 or 6 o'clock in the morning. Because of the poverty and hardships during the difficult times of war, Matins at midnight fell into disuse almost everywhere. Only Kühbach kept it, until the destruction of the convent in 1803. After the midnight hour for Matins was dropped, it was usually begun about 4 o'clock in the morning. The conventual High Mass was about 8 or 9 o'clock, followed by the midday meal. Vespers were held about 2 or 3 o'clock in the afternoon. Five or 6 o'clock was the time for supper; Compline, half an hour later, preceded the night rest.

Meditation was mentioned everywhere as private prayer which lasted half an hour or even an hour, and some statutes recommended the ascetical works of Louis of Granada († 1588) as a meditation book. In summer it was held in the choir and in winter in the warm community room.

The annual retreat of three or four days already belonged to the spiritual exercises. These days were entire days of recollection and prayer, which the individual nuns spent in their cells without conferences being held. In many places the retreat was not held in common, but individually each one chose a time for it. In many convents this exercise was held during Lent. However, the statutes of St. Walburg's in Eichstätt prescribe: "Yearly in the summer time the nuns shall undertake a three day collecting and assembling of the spirit and perform the spiritual exercises under the direction of a priest of the Society of Jesus." They also order that twice a year the nuns make a general confession to a Jesuit priest.

As to the reception of the sacraments, it was ordained that the nuns should go to confession every two weeks and to Holy Communion every month. Every two weeks the confessor was to give an exhortation, and in some convents he also selected the table reading and directed the private retreats by giving subjects for meditation. It is a sign of healthy spirituality that in the statutes the nuns were forbidden under penalty "to draw the veil over the eyes or the mouth in simulated greater recollection."

Work recommended for all was spinning, weaving, sewing, carrying wood and water, kitchen and garden work. When meals were taken in the refectory, the nuns ate in silence and listened to the reader. On feast days they ate in the community room, and there was only a short reading, after which they were allowed to talk. By this time it was customary everywhere to have recreation after the noon meal or after both the noon and evening meals, in some convents only twice a week, in others daily. According to old Roman tradition Thursday was free from work, and on this day in some convents a dispensation from silence was given from the end of Prime until the beginning of Compline. During the recreation period, one could amuse oneself or walk in the garden or play music.

The days of blood-letting, which usually occurred four times a year, continued to be a time for recreation. Then for three days, in St. Walburg's even for an entire week, one could take a rest, receive better food and be dispensed from silence.

Private property, of course, was strictly prohibited, and especially the keeping of dogs, cats, birds and other animals. Concerning this the Kühbach statutes declare: "Since anyone in a convent should have her pastime with none other than Christ, her Spouse, and the little dogs with which ladies in the world amuse themselves should give consecrated persons no recreation but are a nuisance especially in choir and at prayer, so we earnestly desire that, from now on, not a single dog be permitted in the convent or the choir and still less that the nuns themselves carry them around in their arms and place them on a cushion. In this also the abbess shall use discretion so that no one become scandalized over it." The abbess here admonished to discretion was Barbara Stern, who kept three dogs.

The enjoyment of animals was evidently not to be rooted out at Kühbach. At the visitation of 1636 it was confirmed that Abbess Maria von Imhof had dogs, cats, pigeons and other birds, the feeding of which "at the present high prices causes unnecessary expense" in the opinion of the visitators.

The greatest difficulty in the German convents, however, was caused by the strict Tridentine enclosure. For this there was no tradition in Germany. The business of the convent and the position of the abbesses, many of whom belonged to the *Reichstag* or the diet, determined the departures from the convent for the abbess as well as for the nuns. Thus at Kühbach Abbess Barbara Stern declared to the visitors that in summer she had to travel through the fields, that she had vowed to make a pilgrimage three times a year and that occasionally she needed medical treatment. It was also her wish that once in their lifetime all of the choir nuns visit the convents of Hohenwart and Geisenfeld. These convents were respectively 20 and 40 kilometers from Kühbach.

In accord with their instructions from Rome, however, the visitors were adamant on the question of the enclosure. The abbesses were given minute directions as to which doors or windows must be walled up. Permission had to be obtained from the bishop for each departure from the enclosure.

In Geisenfeld, besides the confessor, doctor and craftsmen, the right to enter the enclosure was granted: first, to the bishop, the vicar general and the visitors; second, to members of the Bavarian aristocracy as benefactors of the convent; third, to people of high rank as well as to the parents, brothers and sisters of the choir nuns. They could be shown the convent rooms, but during such a visit all the nuns must remain in their cells.

In Niedernburg at Passau, in keeping with old traditions, the nuns were permitted on the feast of St. Henry the Emperor to go to his chapel in the city "in proper order, as is becoming to religious, and to hold public services there," since St. Henry was considered the second founder of their convent. Conversation in the parlor was carefully regulated too. Thus it was stipulated at Niedernburg that people from the city of Passau could come to the visitors' room only on Tuesdays and Thursdays; strangers, of course, could come on any day. It can be seen from these regulations that the reform statutes did not enforce a complete enclosure but had some consideration for the old German tradition.

A new rite that now appeared in the convent rituals was the solemn clothing at the beginning of the novitiate. The Rule of St. Benedict does not have such a ceremony, since in it the novice receives the religious habit only when he makes his profession, and it is only at this time that he lays aside his secular clothing. The Middle Ages had no clothing ceremony either, as there was scarcely any novitiate. Since the Council of Trent strictly demanded the novitiate, however, the entrance into the novitiate came to be marked with a special rite. There was greater justification for this because there was no postulancy and the entrance into the novitiate actually meant forsaking the world.

The convents for the greater part being for the nobility, the entrance into the convent actually meant the abandoning of earthly pomp, and this was celebrated with the ostentation characteristic of the Baroque period. The novice appeared in all her finery, escorted by a great retinue, placed everything before the altar, and then in the garb of the order, in which she was clothed before the altar, made her entrance into the convent. Sometimes the abbess performed the clothing, but in many convents a prelate performed it in order to increase the solemnity. The pomp soon became so great that the visitators again had to warn against excesses.

It was an innovation at the clothing that the entering novice was given a special monastic name. With few exceptions this was also the case in the post-Tridentine Benedictine congregations. It was an expression of the Marian piety of the time that the nuns used the name of Mary before their conventual name, thus to dedicate themselves to the Mother of God, whose name was henceforth used in the profession document.

Through the influence of the Tridentine reform movement also, the consecration of virgins, which St. Charles Borromeo had rediscovered, so to speak, was returned to the Benedictine convents. Sometimes, according to the old rite, profession was made before the abbess, and later the consecration was bestowed by a bishop. Sometimes profession became a part of the consecration of virgins, and the whole ceremony was performed by the bishop.

Although now as before, the majority of Benedictine convents were under the bishop, still a number strove to unite themselves to the Benedictine congregations now being formed, so as to have stronger support from these. Thus the convents of Alsace joined the Strassburg Congregation, and the convents of Nonnberg, Frauenwörth, Göss and St. George on the Längsee found support through the Salzburg Congregation without being officially accepted into it. The Bursfeld convents took part in the expansion which began anew in the monasteries after the great war.

A good regular life was prevalent throughout the German Benedictine convents of the seventeenth century. It received its characteristic stamp from the piety which was peculiar to the times. Along with choir service the nuns were zealous in honoring the Blessed Sacrament of the altar and the Blessed Virgin. In addition, pious souls found the desired opportunity to express their devotion in the confraternities of a happy death and of the poor souls, in various devotions, in meditation and in the rosary.

In ITALY most of the convents were united to the Cassinese Congregation and followed its manner of life and constitutions. Among those who gave evidence that the spiritual life was flourishing in many of these convents was Blessed Joanna Mary Bonomo († 1670), abbess of Bassano.[4] She was a mystic whose writings on "Rules of the Spiritual Life" and meditations on the Passion exerted great influence.

For the convents of SPAIN which had been united with the congregation of the Claustrales, now in decline, reform constitutions were issued in 1615. These were accepted almost everywhere. From PORTUGAL the first Benedictine convents in South America were founded, and thus the ideal of the contemplative life was brought to Brasil and other South American countries.

It was significant also that in ENGLAND Benedictine nuns again experienced a revival. Since no convents were permitted in England, there was nothing for religiously-inclined young English women to do but to enter convents on the Continent. Soon there arose the understandable desire for the foundation of English convents even outside the homeland.

In Brussels in 1597 the first English convent according to the Rule of St. Benedict was founded, and Mary Percy, daughter of the martyr Thomas Percy, was the first to make her vows there. The founding abbess was Joanna Berkely, who in 1580 had been the first English woman to enter a French convent, St. Peter in Rheims. At the first clothing which she held she gave the habit of St. Benedict to eight young English women. From Brussels foundations were made at Ghent, Dunkirk, Pontoise and Ypres.

Besides these convents which were under the bishops, a second group of convents was formed which was united to the congregation of English Benedictine monks. Directing these young English women, who approached the monks with a petition for affiliation, was 17-year-old GERTRUDE MORE, great granddaughter of St. Thomas More. On Christmas day in 1623 their monastic life

[4]Translator's note: See St. Benedict's English Daughters in Rome, *The Life of Blessed Joanna Mary Bonomo*, Rome 1896.

was begun at Fémy near Cambrai. From Cambrai a convent was founded at Paris.

The noblest flower of the English Benedictine convents was this Gertrude More, who died in 1633 at a youthful age. Under the direction of the eminent master of the spiritual life, Augustine Baker, who was confessor to the convent at Cambrai from 1624 to 1633, Gertrude developed into a mystic of high rank. After her death Augustine Baker released her writings: "Spiritual Exercises" and "Practices of Divine Love."[5]

With their prayers the English Benedictine nuns wished to support the work of the priests in England for reconverting their country to Catholicism. They also took part in this work by accepting young Catholic girls from England into their convents and by conducting boarding schools for girls.

Another great renewal of Benedictine life took place in the convents of POLAND, where the life was almost extinct after the Protestant Revolution and the interior disturbances. The revival here was due to MAGDALENA MORTESKA, whose name deserves to be remembered. She entered Kulm in 1578 and became abbess after only one year. In a short time she succeeded in bringing the convent back to regularity of observance—exact observance, too, of the Rule of St. Benedict, to which the young abbess in her great zeal and her inclination to severity added all kinds of ascetical practices. But instead of frightening candidates away, she attracted a large number of young women by her powerful personality, and under Magdalena the number of nuns in the convent of Kulm rose to 250. Within 20 years 100 novices entered.

From the convent at Kulm others were founded at Lemberg in 1605, Posen in 1608, Jaroslaw and Sondomir in 1611; while Thorn, Graudenz and Schönwald were reformed. From Poland the movement spread to LITHUANIA, where there were convents accepting the observance of Kulm at Wilna, Minsk, Orscha and Smolensk. Pope Clement VIII ratified the constitutions of the Polish Benedictine nuns in 1605. It was unique with this congregation that Magdalena started a seminary for the training of priests. These priests would then serve as confessors in the convents and teach religion in the schools.

---

[5]L. Nolle, *Historische Kommunitäten der Benediktinerinnen in England und ihre Vorfahren im 17. und 18. Jahrhundert*, Stud. u. Mitt. 54, 1936, 433-448.

Translator's note: See *The Holy Practices of a Divine Lover*, London 1909.

The division of Poland was a catastrophe for the Benedictine convents, since in Russia and Prussia they gradually disappeared. The last one in Prussian Poland was closed in 1836, and the last convent of the old Polish Benedictine congregation, the convent of Krozé, came to an end in 1893.

The re-establishment of the Polish state after the First World War benefited the convents also. In 1932 the Benedictine convents of Poland, having reawakened to a new life, formed a congregation preserving the autonomy of the various abbeys under the direction of an abbess president, who presided at the meeting of the general chapter every six years and had the right of visitation. Assisting her was an abbot visitator as counselor.

# CHAPTER 7

DECLINE AND NEW LIFE

About the year 1700 Benedictine monachism had again reached a high peak, and this was followed by a slow decline. There was no corruption but there was a diminishing of strength. The general religious lassitude which marked the period of the Enlightenment and was a phenomenon which gripped the other orders, in fact almost the whole life of the Church, did not stop at the high walls and gratings of the cloister.

In France the religious-ascetical life was greatly hindered by the internal strife of Jansenism, which made itself felt particularly in the sphere of practical asceticism. On the one hand there were unwholesome austerities, a hard rigorism in matters pertaining to confession and reception of the Eucharist, and on the other hand there was a certain laxity.

In Italy and Spain there was a lack of religious life in the convents. They were quite numerous, but in religion and asceticism they were without right guidance, and their strength dwindled more and more.

In a number of German convents the life was determined by their status as imperial and princely institutions. In the Baroque period this meant the penetration of worldly pomp and worldly sentiments. There was no moral decline established here, yet there was an assimilation to the world in many respects. The two principal evils of the past, private ownership and separation from community life, again became noticeable.

We get a picture of the life in a German convent of about 1700 from the statutes which Prince-Abbot Adalbert von Schleifras enacted for the convent at Fulda in 1702. The nuns rose for

Matins at a quarter of an hour before midnight. The prioress or a sister awakened them by knocking on their cells and saying "Venite," which the occupant answered with "Exsultemus." After Matins and Lauds were completed, the nuns again retired, rising about 5:30 for meditation followed by Prime. If for some reason or other it was not possible to rise at night, the nuns were awakened before 4 o'clock to pray Matins and Lauds and to meditate.

After Prime there was manual labor. About 9 o'clock Terce was said, followed at once by the High Mass and Sext. The noon meal about 11 o'clock was the first meal of the day, since breakfast had not yet been introduced. After the noon meal, recreation was held, which was closed by praying None. At 3 o'clock Vespers were sung, and at 5 o'clock the nuns partook of the evening meal, which was again followed by a short recreation period. During both the noon and the evening recreation periods, it was desirable that the conversation be spiritual. At 7 o'clock Compline was prayed, followed by the examination of conscience, and at 8 o'clock the nuns retired.

As a practice of piety in commemoration of the death of our Lord, five *Paters* and *Aves* were prayed and *Tenebrae factae sunt* with its accompanying versicles and oration was sung on Fridays after None. At the beginning of every month a saint's name was drawn as a patron, and at the beginning of the year a special patron for the year. Talking was permitted during the entire day on the feast of St. Martin, on Epiphany and on Shrove Tuesday, yet each time this had to be requested by one of the seniors for the entire convent. On Wednesdays and Saturdays every nun must clean her cell, and on every Saturday the cloister, refectory and dormitories must be cleaned thoroughly.

The rite of profession had taken over many elements from the consecration of virgins, but it emphasized more strongly the entrance into the monastic state, and the preface of the consecration was omitted. Profession was made before the prince-abbot or his representative.

The profession formula read: "I, Sister N., born in the city of N., give and offer myself as an eternal spouse and constant handmaid to Jesus Christ, my Lord and Savior, to His honorable Mother, the most Blessed Virgin Mary, to our holy father Benedict, to all the beloved saints and especially to our holy patrons

Boniface, Sturmius, Elizabeth and other saints. In virtue of this document, after due deliberation, I promise and vow before God and His dear Mother and all the beloved saints in the presence of Lord N., the most reverend prince and lord abbot of Fulda, lord chancellor of the Roman empress, primate of Gaul and Germany, and in the presence of the Reverend Lady Prioress N., and you beloved sisters here present, conversion of my life and morals, stability in all that is good; I vow and promise especially voluntary poverty, perpetual chastity and complete obedience according to the Rule of the aforementioned holy father Benedict, in the name of God the Father and the Son and the Holy Spirit. Amen. As a true record and for further confirmation of the above-mentioned vows I have written this document with my own hand, 1700 years and N. days after the birth of Jesus Christ our Lord and Savior."

The profession formula at the beginning of the Thirty Years' War was still in Latin, but after the war it was in German, evidently because not all the nuns were sufficiently well versed in the Latin language, a result of the general cultural decline of the times.

For the manner of making profession before an abbess we have the report of Frater Henry of the monastery of Kremsmünster, who as a student in Salzburg witnessed the celebration of a profession on January 29, 1746, in the convent of Nonnberg. He recounted: "Early this morning I, with several others, went to the convent of Nonnberg because a nun was making profession, which not only I could see but anyone of either sex who wanted to. The profession was made in the loft of their choir; the father confessor therefore opened the door to let us go up. We entered the choir loft, where we saw a number of nuns already kneeling in their choir cloaks (cucullas). Finally, the abbess also came into the choir wearing a crown of silver and gold like an emperor. She seated herself in her chair and three choir nuns stood near her with crozier, book and ceremonial staff.

"When she was thus seated, the *neoprofessa* wearing a white veil went up to her, and the abbess embraced her, saying nothing. The other choir nuns did the same as she was led to each one by the prioress and the novice mistress. After this the abbess prayed some Latin orations aloud. Then the *neoprofessa* prostrated herself and the litany of All Saints was sung, led by two choir nuns.

At its conclusion the novice mistress went to her and stamped her foot, saying: 'Arise, you who sleep. Your spouse will make you happy.' Finally she rose from the floor, and several orations were prayed as before.

"Then she was divested of her clothing, though not entirely, since one could not yet see her bare head. Eventually, the abbess took the shears and cut off a small lock of hair, which stood out from the completely shorn head and which must have been allowed to grow perhaps the entire year, in the manner of the pandours, saying these words: 'We wish to take from you your worldliness with the cutting of your curly hair.' Even if the hair stood out like a broomstick she must call it 'your curly hair.' The abbess also read many other texts at the divesting; and God knows how many caps the *neoprofessa* wore, for I counted three white ones, and each time the abbess said: 'May the Lord take from you the old man.'

"After the removal of the old clothing she was invested with the habit of profession with the words 'May the Lord clothe you with the new man.' Over the white veil she was also given a black veil of the same size. Then she had to go toward the middle and make her profession, singing three times in Latin 'Suscipe me Domine,' and the others responded with the same words. She then commenced her profession in German: 'In the name of the Most Holy Trinity. Amen. I, Sister Mary Celestine Victoria of Francis de Sales . . .' When she finished she had to go once more to the abbess, who placed a beautiful wreath on her head and also put her bridegroom in her arms, a nicely adorned crucifix, and lastly placed the ring on her finger. *Et finis est.*"

The so-called cell bridegroom mentioned here was either a crucifix or the Infant of Prague, adorned with clothing, which served as a remembrance of profession. It was given a place of honor in the cell and was provided with new clothing every year.

From the horarium of Fulda in 1700 we can see that the nuns strove for a good monastic life and probably lived it too. Yet the same statutes say that every nun received from the convent only the general fare, while she herself must provide for everything else, even clothing.

This was done through the *peculium*. At a nun's entrance into the convent, the parents left a specified sum for her with the cellarer, and this could be increased occasionally through further

deposits. Aside from the monastic habit the nun paid for everything she needed, such as shoes, gloves and other useful little
articles, out of this sum. Monthly she received from this amount
the pocket money, with which she could buy sweets, tea, coffee,
and even snuff, a favorite with the ladies at that time. These ex-
penditures she noted down on a slip of paper, which she turned
over at the end of the month to the "gracious lady," her abbess,
so that there was a certain control. This was an abuse but it was
sanctioned.

Thus a rather pleasant manner of life had penetrated into the
convents, with little striving for higher perfection and no high
aspirations. Music was a favorite pastime in the convent. In the
guest room there were nice little social gatherings and coffee parties,
and the "gracious lady" held "court" in her prelature, to which
the nuns were also invited.

The menu which was placed before the convent visitators at
Kühbach at the visitation of July 27, 1737, tells us something of
the fare of the German convents of the Baroque period: "On
Sunday noon, soup, an appetizer, meat, cabbage, fried meat
(Gebratenes) and rice soup. In the evening, salad, fried meat
and barley (Gersten). On Monday noon, soup, appetizer, cabbage
and barley. In the evening, soup or salad, preserved meat and
barley. On Tuesday noon, soup, appetizer, meat, cabbage, barley.
In the evening, salad, fried meat and barley. On Wednesday
noon, soup, dumplings (Mehlspeise), cabbage and other green
garden vegetables or dried fruit. In the evening, soup, fresh eggs,
prunes or dried fruit. Thursday noon, soup, appetizer, meat,
cabbage and barley. In the evening, salad, fried meat and barley.
Friday noon, soup, dumplings, cabbage and another vegetable.
In the evening, soup. Saturday noon, soup, puree or mush, cabbage and another vegetable. In the evening, soup. On a feast day
which is a meat day: soup, appetizer, meat or chicken pie, large
or small, goose or chicken, almond or fruit cake or other desserts.
In the evening, salad, preserves, roast duck and a dessert. At noon
on an abstinence day, soup, fish, pastry and dessert. In the evening,
salad, soup, fish, some pastry and wine sauce."

The food was plentiful, then, but very monotonous. It must
be remembered, too, that there were many fast days. Besides the
40 days of Lent, there was fasting on all Fridays except in Easter-
tide as well as on Mondays, Wednesdays, Fridays and Saturdays

in Advent. On all these days there was only one hot meal and no meat.

The un-Christian spirit of the period of the Enlightenment brought in its wake another decline in the number of nuns in the convents. In the German convents there were in general scarcely 30 members, and fewer still in the convents of Italy and Spain. In France too there were many small convents. When the Blessed Marie Rose de Loye, who died as a martyr in 1794, entered the convent at Caderousse in 1761, there were only two nuns, and it was a great achievement of Abbess de Tilly that under her the number rose to 15.

The French Revolution and the German secularization thrust a rough hand into this quiet convent life of the Baroque period. In France all the convents were dissolved in a most brutal manner, many nuns were imprisoned and many perished miserably. All convents and churches were plundered and robbed of their valuable treasures, and some were also partially destroyed or devastated. Only ruins remained.

Less cruel but nevertheless bitter was the fate of the convents in Germany. By a decree of the imperial deputation of 1803 all imperial and prince abbeys were dissolved and the other convents, which did not have such a rank, fell to the princes as compensation for their losses. Some convents in Austria, some in Switzerland, and very few in Germany itself withstood the general destruction. Among the latter was St. Mary in Fulda. All these convents, however, had to struggle for their existence. To make a living they had to take over schools, and one could scarcely speak of a monastic life in the old sense.

The dissolution also spread over Poland, Italy, Spain and Portugal. At the beginning of the nineteenth century there were only a few convents remaining as witnesses of a great past.

But the same century witnessed an unexpected resurgence, the revival of old convents, the founding of new abbeys inspired by the old monastic idea, the formation of new congregations in keeping with the Rule of St. Benedict, and the foundation of convents in North America, Australia and Africa.

In the first place this indestructible vitality showed itself in those abbeys which stemmed from the old period. After the period of the Enlightenment the venerable old convent of Nonnberg in Salzburg was the first to renew the inner life and, touched by the living breath of Catholic romanticism, to revive its powers so that it could transmit new life to other places. Some of the old convents in Bavaria rose again too, after the frightful storm had passed and King Louis I, the great friend and patron of Benedictinism, had again established the convent life. These were Frauenwörth in Chiemsee, St. Walburg in Eichstätt, and Tettenweis in lower Bavaria.

The nuns of St. Walburg remained as pensioners in their convent, which was considered closed. Their fidelity was rewarded, since there were still nine of them living at the restoration of the monastic life in 1825 when novices could again be received. When in 1848 the last nun of the old period died, the convent already had 25 nuns. In Switzerland there was also new life in the convents of Sarnen and Fahr.

Along with the old convents, which maintained a certain union with their earlier observance, there were also abbeys which accepted a new way and created an observance that preferred to start from the traditions of the early Middle Ages. For this formation they were indebted to the two great monastic movements, Solesmes and Beuron. These set as their goal the renewal of monasticism by joining the essential elements of the Rule of St. Benedict with the oldest traditions.

Both Abbot Prosper Guéranger († 1875) and Archabbot Maurus Wolter († 1890) gave loving attention to the convents. They were interested in the foundation of these convents, believing that the ideals they wanted to bring into reality could be lived most purely in the convents. In contrast to the monks, the nuns were removed from priestly duties and care of souls. Near Solesmes Dom Prosper Guéranger founded the convent of St. Cecile, which began a brilliant career. When the convents in France were dissolved as a result of the persecution of the Church, convents of this new observance were founded in England, and one in Holland at Oosterhout.

Besides convents of the new observance there were also some which sprang from convents of the old French observance, notably the one at Pradines, whose foundress was Marie Thérèse de Bavoz († 1883). She formed a congregation under the name of the Benedictine Nuns of the Heart of Mary and combined the contemplative life with the work of educating young girls.

In France there arose also the Congregation of Missionary

Benedictine Nuns, a foundation by Dom J. M. Besse of the abbey of Ligugé and Madame Wadington-Delmas, at Vanves (Seine), which combines the contemplative with the active life. The congregation now has houses in the French colonies and is affiliated with the Cassinese Congregation of the Primitive Observance.

After the pattern of St. Cecile at Solesmes the Beuronese Benedictine Congregation erected the convent of St. Gabriel in Prague, whose nuns had to flee from Bohemia in 1918 and settled at Bertholdstein in Styria. Other foundations which followed were Maredret in Belgium, St. Hildegard in Eibingen, Kellenried in Württemberg and Holy Cross at Herstelle on the Weser. The Beuronese observance was accepted also by Frauenwörth in Chiemsee and more recently by St. Mary's in Fulda, Mariendonk near Kempen and Varensell in Westphalia. Drawing inspiration from the same source were such convents as Ermeton in Belgium and Alexanderdorf in the electorate of Brandenburg, which seek to unite a certain amount of external activity with the contemplative life.

The secularization also led to the suppression of the English Benedictine convents on the Continent, but by this time the Benedictine nuns of these houses could return to their homeland. In this manner England again received those monastic establishments to which it owed its Christian culture. The convent of Cambrai was transferred to Stanbrook, Brussels to East Bergholt, Ghent to Sulton, Paris to Colwich, Dunkirk to Teignmouth; and in 1914 the convent of Ypres, which had remained unmolested, was transferred to Kyllmore, Ireland.

In 1852 some nuns[1] from St. Walburg founded the convent of St. Joseph in North America at St. Marys, Elk County, Pennsylvania, and so the ideal of the contemplative life was brought to the New World. The first prioress of this North American Benedictine convent was Benedicta Riepp († 1862). There followed the foundation of St. Benedict at Erie and others.

Shortly before this, Australia had received its first Benedictine convent, called New Subiaco, through Archbishop Polding. The nineteenth century likewise witnessed a resurgence of the convents in Italy and Spain. In South America also, Benedictine

---

[1]Translator's note: Two choir nuns and one lay sister arrived in New York on July 4, 1852, from St. Walburg, Eichstätt, which subsequently sent nine more members for the American foundation.

convents which enjoyed great prestige were founded, in Brasil, Argentina and Chile.

The convents of Perpetual Adoration, which recovered from the effects of the French Revolution sooner than other convents did, enjoyed a great expansion in the nineteenth century. Even in the midst of the general chaos courageous nuns began the life of atonement again in 1796 in a private house in Paris. Another community was formed at Caen in 1804, and one at Toul in 1806. After 1816 the nuns were again permitted to wear the monastic garb. In 1814 the princess of Bourbon-Condé started an adoration convent near the Temple prison in Paris, which became a flourishing foundation. Among the French convents the one at Arras held first place, wielding enough influence to make numerous new foundations. The first nuns of Perpetual Adoration came to Germany in 1854, establishing convents at Trier, Bonn and Osnabrück. They came to Italy in 1878, to Spain in 1904, and today they are found almost everywhere in the world, including North and South America.

The nuns of Calvary also experienced an increase in numbers, but their expansion was slower than that of the nuns of Perpetual Adoration.

A proof of the new strength of the Benedictine life and a sign of the attraction which the Rule of St. Benedict and the monastic ideal again exercised is the number of COMMUNITIES OF SISTERS based on the Rule of our saint which came into existence in the nineteenth century. First to be mentioned here are the Benedictines of Maria Rickenbach in Switzerland, founded in 1857 by Abbot Anselm Villiger of Engelberg († 1901). They unite perpetual adoration with teaching. From Maria Rickenbach the sisters came to North America in 1875, where their first foundation was St. Scholastica in Clyde, Missouri. This convent became famous through the great charitable work of its spiritual director, Father Lukas Etlin († 1927) in the time of need after the first World War. Foundations followed at Mount Angel, Oregon, and Yankton and Sturgis in South Dakota.

In France the Benedictine Sisters of the Poor were founded in 1872 by Dom Camille Leduc of the Congregation of Solesmes. In Belgium the Oblate Sisters of St. Benedict were established at Heverlé in 1904. The Adorers of the Heart of Jesus, whose motherhouse is at Tyburn, England, were founded at Montmartre in

1897 by Adèle Garnier, Mother Mary of St. Peter († 1924).[2] In Australia, Archbishop Polding founded the Benedictine Sisters of the Good Samaritan in 1857. In Germany the Missionary Sisters of Tutzing, who have numerous convents in mission countries, were associated at the start with the Benedictine Congregation of St. Ottilien (1885).[3] In 1927 the community of Lioba Sisters was founded at Freiburg in Breisgau, and in more recent times a Benedictine community was started at Alexanderdorf in the electorate of Brandenburg.[4]

Congregations formed in North America[5] included that of St. Scholastica[6] at Atchison, Kansas (1922), with a number of convents and academies, and the Congregation of Perpetual Adoration at Clyde, Missouri (1925).

The organization of the Benedictine nuns is looser than that of the monks. While all the monasteries for monks are united into congregations at the head of which is the abbot primate in Rome, there are many communities of Benedictine nuns that do not belong to a congregation. For the women religious of the Benedictine order there are convents of nuns and communities of sisters. The nuns *(moniales, monachae)* maintain choir prayer, have a strict enclosure, make solemn vows and sometimes also have the consecration of virgins.[7] The communities of sisters make only simple vows and do not have a strict enclosure; they do not chant the entire monastic Office, and they do perform external works.[8]

[2]Translator's note: See The Nuns of Tyburn Convent, *Tyburn Hill of Glory*, London 1953.

[3]Translator's note: The *Catalogus Familiarum Confoederatarum O.S.B.*, 1955, now lists the Congregation of Sisters for Foreign Missions of Tutzing as being founded in 1885 and erected as a congregation directly under the Holy See in 1924; see p. 517.

[4]Translator's note: Alexanderdorf was founded in 1930. *Catalogus*, p. 530.

[5]Translator's note: For a complete list of congregations in North America in 1955 see Appendix, part III.

[6]Translator's note: See Sister Mary Regina Baska, O.S.B., *The Benedictine Congregation of St. Scholastica: Its Foundation and Development (1852-1930)*, Washington 1935.

[7]Translator's note: On October 24, 1950, the Sacred Congregation of Religious granted the reception of Consecration of Virgins to the Benedictine Sisters of the United States. The ceremony may be performed either by bishops of the United States or by abbots of the Benedictine Order in this country.

[8]Translator's note: See Appendix, Part III, to learn something of the kind and extent of the external works performed by the Benedictine Sisters of the United States at the present time.

The convents of nuns form the following groups:

1) convents of nuns directly under the Apostolic See; these are the Congregation of Calvary and individual abbeys of the old observance;

2) convents of nuns which belong to a Benedictine congregation and are subject to an abbot, as for example the Beuronese Benedictine convents of Eibingen, Herstelle and Bertholdstein; Fahr, Sarnen, Seedorf and Au in Switzerland; Stanbrook and Colwich in England; Sao Paolo in Brasil; Frosinone and Subiaco in Italy;

3) convents of nuns which are under the bishops, like Nonnberg, St. Walburg in Eichstätt, Frauenwörth in Chiemsee and St. Mary in Fulda. To this group belong most of the convents in Spain, more than 30, and close to 80 in Italy.

To a fourth group belong the communities of sisters just mentioned.

Finally, in most recent times, there are communities of sisters without vows, striving to pattern their life according to the Rule of St. Benedict.

Thus the ideal of St. Benedict is lived by a large number of women all over the world at the present time; it is actually lived in the old traditional manner in the convents for nuns, and in a new manner by the various congregations of sisters. Even if the communities of sisters do not say the entire psalmody, yet they are guided by the principles of the Rule of St. Benedict and base their piety and asceticism on that school which is the school of the Lord's service.

As formerly, the nuns again support the work of the monks with their quiet prayer. The monks, who have found their way back to the ideal of the old monastic life, also transmit the treasures of the liturgical monastic life to the sisters. Thus "the enclosed garden" of the convents at the present time is full of glorious blossoms and rich fruit. Intellectual activity—as evidenced by the literature emanating from the various abbeys—and artistic creation are flourishing once more.

The influx to the convents of St. Benedict is growing steadily. The convents of St. Cecile near Solesmes, Stanbrook in England, Maredret in Belgium, Nonnberg in Austria, St. Walburg at Eichstätt, St. Hildegard at Eibingen, Herstelle on the Weser and St. Mary at Fulda, to name only a few, are held in high esteem and have become examples of the monastic ideal as it is lived by women in complete devotion and purity.[9]

Like the monasteries, the convents also live the Benedictine ideal, but each in its own way. Every convent has its own traditions and its own customs, but all are united by their love for the Rule of St. Benedict, their zeal for the psalmody and their esteem for the contemplative way in silence, reading and work.

In Benedictine convents today the following horarium is usual. Matins are no longer said during the night or in the early morning, but are anticipated at about 8 p.m. Then begins the night rest, which ends in the morning about 5:30. Lauds and Prime are then said. The conventual High Mass at about 7 o'clock is preceded by Terce. Sext and None follow at midday and Vespers —always sung—around 6. Once a day, time is set aside for private prayer, reading and meditation. Once or twice a week the spiritual director holds a conference in the field of exegesis or liturgy, and every Sunday an exhortation on ascetical matters is given by the abbess.

Just as the monastic life of the men is naturally affected by the activity of the newer orders of priests, so the monastic life of women is also affected, especially by the sisters of charity, the teaching and missionary sisters. Over against the ideal of the sister who is active in the world, the ideal of the nun living hidden in the convent has yielded ground until it is seldom even considered and hardly understood. Before the Protestant Revolution, Germany had more than 100 abbeys of Benedictine nuns and more than 200 abbeys of Cistercian nuns; now it has only 10 Benedictine and 7 Cistercian abbeys of nuns, to which must be added some Benedictine convents of Perpetual Adoration. This small number stands in contrast to the large number of communities of sisters.

There is a widespread opinion that the time of the contemplative communities is past and it is more important today to relieve exterior needs than to bury oneself in contemplation. No one will overlook these needs and deem it unimportant to serve the sick, the poor and the children. But besides hospitals, homes for the

[9]Translator's note: This list of convents with a good reputation might well be extended to include many of the convents of the Benedictine Sisters in the United States. Regina Laudis, Bethlehem, Connecticut, and the Congregation of Sisters of Perpetual Adoration, Clyde, Missouri, undoubtedly fulfill the monastic ideal of the contemplative life in a most wholesome manner.

aged and schools for the children, we need houses of God and particularly such as are filled with the incense of prayer and psalmody. An *Orante,* a virgin lifting her hands in prayer, is the picture by which the Church has represented herself in the catacombs.

Today also nothing is more necessary than prayer, and the time of the old monastic orders is by no means past. The more the world loses its sanctity, the more man becomes engrossed in the present life and its activities, the more important it is that there be a state in which the Lord alone is served, that there be women who guard the Mystery and walk in the Spirit. "The undivided service" in perfect surrender and retirement is more necessary today than ever as a symbol and a plea for mankind fallen away from Christ.

If the lamps which the virgins awaiting the Lord carry in their hands were extinguished, and if the holy psalmody were silenced, then it would be night, and darkness would usurp power over the world. God's Holy Spirit, who keeps creating life in His Church, has in our days reawakened love of the contemplative ideal and of the performance of the divine praise. The old monasticism has shown its vital strength in the fact that so many virgins entrust themselves to the Rule of St. Benedict, to this school of the Lord's service, and in this school learn to prefer nothing to the service of God.

May this virginal light, which the love of Christ has enkindled anew, dispel the darkness of our time, and may the bridal song of love surge up in psalmody above all the noise of a world estranged from God to the throne of the Trinity, for His glory, for the salvation of the world!

# *Appendix*

## NUNS AND SISTERS OF THE ORDER OF SAINT
## BENEDICT IN 1955

Father Hilpisch concludes his book with a list of German convents, which is omitted here. For it, there has been substituted
a series of tabulations, summaries and diagrams to give a com-
prehensive view of the status of Benedictine women not only
in Germany but in all countries.

The distinction between nuns and sisters has not always been
clearly defined and understood. In fact, ordinary usage in the
United States does not recognize such a distinction. Canon 488
No. 7 of canon law does state that sisters are "religious women
with simple vows; nuns, religious with solemn vows or, unless
it appears otherwise from the nature of the case or from the
context, religious women whose vows are normally solemn, but
which by a disposition of the Holy See, are simple in certain
regions."[1] The *Catalogus Familiarum Confoederatarum, O.S.B.*[2]
adds that nuns observe papal enclosure and pray the monastic
Office while sisters observe episcopal enclosure and pray part of
the monastic Office or the Little Office of the Blessed Virgin.

Despite these definitions, there seem to be many exceptions to
the rule. For example, the members of the Congregation of the
Immaculate Conception of Poland made simple vows and had
episcopal enclosure and yet have the rights and privileges of
nuns and are classed as nuns directly under the Holy See in the
tabulation of the *Catalogus.* Similarly, the members of the Convent of St. Walburg, Eichstätt, make simple vows and have a

[1]Canonical Legislation concerning Religious, Authorized English Translation,
(Westminster, Md. 1948) p. 8.

[2]All statistical information given in the tables of this Appendix was collected
and tabulated from the 1955 edition of the *Catalogus,* pp. 485-539, supplemented
by current data from *The Official Catholic Directory,* 1957 edition.

rather strict episcopal enclosure, but by special indult they are classed as nuns under the local ordinary.

Sometimes the members of a community are listed as nuns by one classification and as sisters by another. For example, the *Catalogus* lists the community of Regina Laudis of Bethlehem, Connecticut, as sisters under the local ordinary, while the 1956 Catholic Directory for the United States lists them as Benedictine Nuns of Primitive Observance. The fact is that at present the members of this convent make simple vows and have episcopal enclosure, but they look forward to the time when the first wing of their abbey and enclosure walls will be erected, so that they can request solemn vows and pontifical enclosure.

The Benedictine sisters in the United States make simple vows and have episcopal enclosure. For the most part, the entire monastic Office is chanted in choir, at least in the motherhouses of the various communities, while in dependent houses all of the Divine Office except Matins is recited in choir. Since 1950 the privilege of the ceremony of Consecration of Virgins, generally reserved for nuns, has been granted to the Benedictine sisters of North America.

The following table[3] gives some interesting comparisons between nuns and sisters.

### NUNS

| | Monas-teries | Choir Nuns | Lay Sisters | Externs | Novices | Total Religious |
|---|---|---|---|---|---|---|
| Subject to: | | | | | | |
| Holy See | 15 | 225 | 130 | 19 | 49 | 423 |
| Regular Prelate | 21 | 700 | 315 | 44 | 84 | 1143 |
| Local Ordinary | 211 | 4778 | 2296 | 267 | 586 | 7927 |
| | 247 | 5703 | 2741 | 330 | 719 | 9493 |

### SISTERS

| | Monas-teries | Dependent Houses | Sisters | Novices | Total Religious |
|---|---|---|---|---|---|
| Subject to: | | | | | |
| Holy See | 77 | 267 | 7,343 | 315 | 7,658 |
| Regular Prelate | 2 | - - - | 85 | 8 | 93 |
| Local Ordinary | 41 | 122 | 3,087 | 267 | 3,354 |
| | 120 | 389 | 10,515 | 590 | 11,105 |

[3]There are some discrepancies between the sums of this table and the tabulations of the following parts of the Appendix. Nevertheless, a good general picture is presented.

None of the 9493 nuns are located in the United States whereas 6963 of the 11,105 Benedictine sisters, or almost 63%, do live in this country. An interesting fact revealed by this table is that only 4% of the nuns are directly subject to the Holy See whereas 69% of the sisters are directly under papal jurisdiction. It is evidently much more common for European houses to be subject to the local ordinary than is the case with the American convents. About 84% of the nuns and only about 30% of all the sisters are subject to the local ordinary.

Although the Benedictine sisters have been in the United States only a little over 100 years, more than 37% of the total number of women living according to the Rule of St. Benedict today are located in this country. In 1852 when Mother Benedicta Riepp[4] and her two companions came to Pennsylvania from St. Walburg's convent in Eichstätt, they were the only women following the Rule of St. Benedict in this country. Today there are 6963; not all of these, however, have sprung from the first Eichstätt foundation, as the charts[5] given in Part IV of this Appendix indicate.

Part I below summarizes the data on Benedictine nuns, their congregations, location of convents, date of founding, number of members and name of foundress when known. Part II gives similar information for sisters, listing the number of schools and pupils, and also the number of hospitals and patients. A study of the information contained in these two sections gives an over-all picture of religious women living under the Rule of St. Benedict today.

The information contained in the last two parts of this Appendix is restricted to North America. Part III gives rather detailed information concerning the 4 congregations of the United States and also the 4 convents under local ordinary. The convent at Norfolk, Nebraska, will be found under the congregation of Sisters for Foreign Missions. Their general motherhouse is at Tutzing, Bavaria, but a provincial motherhouse is located at Norfolk. The convent of Boulder, Colorado, is dependent upon

[4]For the life and work of Mother Benedicta in North America see Sister M. Grace MacDonald, O.S.B., *With Lamps Burning* (St. Joseph, Minnesota, 1957), pp. 8-19.
[5]These charts are similar to the ones appearing in *Spring and Harvest*, (St. Meinrad, Indiana, 1952), p. 46-47.

the motherhouse in Eichstätt but is a canonically erected priory with its own novitiate.

The Catholic Directory for the United States for 1956 reveals that 9 colleges, about 100 high schools and academies, and more than 500 grade schools are conducted by the Benedictine sisters of this country. Some communities conduct schools for under-privileged children and some have charge of orphanages. There is practically no way of recording the amount of catechetical work done during the summer months, on Saturdays and in released-time classes. Active work is done in the foreign mission field as well as in the home missions among the Indians and Negroes. The sisters conduct nearly 50 hospitals, a number of homes for the aged, and rest homes.

Besides doing school and hospital work the sisters are engaged in such activities as making vestments, preparing altar breads and making candles. Some communities are engaged in printing and publishing. A number of sisters have done creative writing of high quality; others have produced original work in the arts. One sister under the auspices of the Smithsonian Institute has made a fine contribution to the study of the Indian of both North and South America.

Part IV presents the geographical location of the North American foundations by tabulation and map; the chronological order in which they were made; and the European ancestry of these foundations. The rapid spread of Benedictinism in this country is portrayed graphically by the chart showing the nine daughter houses founded from St. Marys, Pennsylvania, and all the subsequent foundations made from these.

In general the establishment of convents followed the German immigration. The states which have no Benedictine convents are located chiefly in the three regions of New England, southeastern United States, and the Rocky Mountain area. Twenty-one states do not have a single Benedictine motherhouse, as compared with 27 in which there are one or more.

## PART I

# NUNS

## A. NUNS DIRECTLY SUBJECT TO THE HOLY SEE

### 1) Nuns of OUR LADY AT CALVARY (France)

The congregation originated with the monastic reform at Fontevrault and was approved by the Holy See in 1621. Besides following the Rule of St. Benedict, the nuns practice special devotion to the Passion of our Lord. A superior general with her council rules the congregation. Each house has its own novitiate. Seven monasteries are located in France and one in Jerusalem on Mount Olivet.

Monasteries 8; Choir nuns 108; Lay sisters 41; Auxiliaries 13; Novices 17.

### 2) Congregation of the IMMACULATE CONCEPTION (Poland)

(Since it was impossible to obtain more recent information, data from the 1950 edition was reprinted.)

The congregation was erected by the Sacred Congregation of Religious in 1932. Each monastery preserves its autonomy. The congregation is ruled by an abbess president and two abbess assistants. The congregation is given an abbot visitator nominated by the Holy See from among the Benedictine abbots. He makes a canonical visitation every six years. Although the members make only simple vows and have episcopal enclosure, they have the rights and privileges of nuns.

Monasteries 7; Choir nuns 117; Lay sisters 89; Novices 36; Extern sisters 2.

## B. NUNS SUBJECT TO A REGULAR PRELATE

These monasteries are subject to an abbot or to a congregation of Benedictine monks. Monasteries of this type are located in Italy, Austria, Brasil, Argentina, Germany, Switzerland, Belgium and England. There are none in the United States or Canada.

Examples of this type are:

| Monastery | Location | Subject to: |
|-----------|----------|-------------|
| St. Scholastica | Buenos Aires, Argentina | Archabbot of Brasilian Congregation |
| St. Scholastica | Cassino, Italy | Abbot Ordinary of Monte Cassino |
| Holy Cross | Herstelle, Germany | Congregation of Beuron |
| St. John the Baptist | Maredret, Belgium | Belgian Congregation |
| Blessed Virgin Mary | Stanbrook, England | Abbot President of English Congregation |

Monasteries 21; Choir nuns 700; Lay sisters 315; Novices 84; Extern Sisters 44.

## C. NUNS SUBJECT TO THE LOCAL ORDINARY

### *Nuns United Into Congregations*

a) Nuns of PERPETUAL ADORATION OF THE BLESS-ED SACRAMENT

This congregation was founded by Mother Mechtild de Bar in the seventeenth century. The nuns make simple vows. Besides following the Rule of St. Benedict, the nuns observe perpetual adoration of the Blessed Sacrament. Each monastery is autonomous and is ruled by a prioress. Monasteries are located in Italy, France, Germany, Holland, Luxembourg, Belgium, Scotland and Argentina.

Monasteries 43; Nuns 1030; Lay sisters 742; Novices 154; Extern sisters and oblates 35

b) Nuns of the MOST PURE HEART OF MARY (France)

These monasteries were restored after the French revolution by D. Placida Theresia de Bavoz. Now they are united into a federation formed according to the norms of the apostolic constitution "Sponsa Christi." The statutes were approved by the Holy See in 1953. There are six monasteries, all located in France—at Chantelle, Jouarre, La Rochette, Pradines, St. Jean d'Angely, and Flee.

Monasteries 6; Nuns 258; Regular oblates 44; Lay sisters 61; Novices and postulants 22.

c) Nuns of the EUCHARISTIC KING (Philippine Islands)

There is only one monastery in this congregation at Vigan, Philippine Islands, founded in 1931 and made an abbey in 1950.

The convent of Mary of Peace at Kirchsletten, Germany, founded in 1953, is dependent upon the monastery at Vigan.

Mission Stations 7; Choir nuns 17; Novices 5; Professed active sisters 2; Novices 36; Postulants 10; Oblates 18; Oblate novices 3.

## Nuns Not United Into Congregations

The following tabulation of monasteries was made by classifying them according to the countries in which they are located. Among the French monasteries are such outstanding ones as Faremoutiers, Lisieux, Poitiers, Solesmes, and five which belong to the Cassinese Congregation of Primitive Observance. The six monasteries of Germany are located at Eichstätt, Frauenchiemsee, Fulda, Kempen-Mariendonk, Tettenweis and Varensell. The monastery of Rijeka, Croatia, is in exile in Italy. It is, however, counted among the 9 monasteries of Croatia, but no statistics were available as to the number of religious.

| Country | Monasteries | Nuns | Lay Sisters | Novices | Extern Sisters |
|---|---|---|---|---|---|
| Austria | 1 | 46 | 40 | 2 | |
| Belgium | 11 | 309 | 72 | 13 | 4 |
| Brasil | 1 | 17 | 2 | 6 | |
| Canada | 2 | 59 | 10 | 16 | 4 |
| Croatia (Jugoslavia) | 9 | 68 | 21 | 14 | |
| Denmark | 1 | 24 | | 3 | |
| England | 10 | 229 | 106 | 20 | 2 |
| France | 15 | 594 | 194 | 59 | 29 |
| Germany | 6 | 259 | 265 | 53 | |
| Holland | 2 | 69 | 26 | 11 | |
| Italy | 76 | 1210 | 566 | 151 | 1 |
| Spain | 25 | 550 | 189 | | |
| Switzerland | 2 | 30 | 17 | 2 | |

## PART II

# SISTERS

## A. SISTERS DIRECTLY SUBJECT TO THE HOLY SEE

1) Sisters of the CONGREGATION OF ST. SCHOLASTICA (U.S.)

This congregation was approved by the Holy See in 1922 and is ruled by a superior general, elected every six years from the prioresses of the congregation. Each monastery maintains its own chapter, novitiate and administration. The sisters are occupied chiefly in teaching. Since the data was tabulated two new monasteries have become a part of this congregation: St. Lucy's Priory, Glendora, California, and St. Scholastica's Convent, San Antonio, Texas.

Monasteries 15; Dependent houses 32; Sisters 2325; Novices 90; Schools 238; Pupils 68,983; Hospitals 6; Patients 24,080.

2) Congregation of SISTERS FOR FOREIGN MISSIONS (Bavaria)

Founded in 1865 in Tutzing, Bavaria, it was erected as a congregation in 1924. The congregation is ruled by a superior general residing at Grottaferrata, Rome. Monasteries are located in Italy, Germany, Africa, Philippine Islands, Brasil, Japan, Korea, Bulgaria and Immaculata Convent at Norfolk, Nebraska (Norfolk has 68 sisters, 3 schools and 3 hospitals). The sisters of the congregation do school and hospital work along with their missionary work.

Monasteries 14; Sisters 1163; Novices 31.

3) Congregation of the SISTERS OF PERPETUAL ADORATION (U.S.)

The monastery at Clyde, Missouri, was founded in 1874 by sisters from Maria Rickenbach. It flourished especially by the work of Rev. Lucas Etlin, monk of Blessed Virgin Mary Abbey of Conception, Missouri. The congregation was erected by the

Holy See in 1925 and is ruled by a superior general residing at Clyde. Each monastery is entitled "Benedictine Convent of Perpetual Adoration" but has a special patron. The novitiate for the congregation is at Clyde.

Monasteries 5; Sisters 271; Novices 10; Oblates 11; Postulants 10.

## 4) Congregation of the ADORERS OF THE SACRED HEART OF JESUS of Montmartre

The congregation was founded in 1898 by M. Maria of St. Peter (Adèle Garnier), prescribing perpetual adoration of the Blessed Sacrament. The congregation was approved by the Holy See in 1930 and is ruled by a superior general who resides at Tyburn, London. Another convent is located at Royston, England, and the third one in Brussels, Belgium.

Monasteries 3; Choir sisters 46; Lay sisters 17; Novices 3.

## 5) Congregation of SAINT GERTRUDE THE GREAT (U.S.)

The congregation was approved in 1937 and is ruled by a prioress general, chosen for six years from among the prioresses of the congregation. Each priory forms its own monastic family, has its own novitiate and administration. The sisters do educational and hospital work.

Monasteries 9; Dependent houses 222; Sisters 1633; Novices 65; Schools 199; Pupils 27,725; Hospitals 23; Patients 56,524; Orphanage 1; Orphans 29; Homes for aged 3; Patients 112.

## 6) Congregation of SAINT BENEDICT (U.S.)

The congregation was erected in 1947 and received final pontifical approbation in 1956. It is ruled by a mother president and her council. Each priory has its own novitiate and administration. The sisters do both educational and hospital work.

Monasteries 6; Sisters 1551; Novices 86; Schools 103; Pupils 27,832; Hospitals 8; Patients 41,837.

## 7) Congregation of the SISTERS "SERVANTS OF THE POOR"

Founded in Angers in 1872 by Rev. Camille Leduc, monk of St. Peter, Solesmes, it received the Decree of Praise in 1887 but remained under diocesan jurisdiction until 1928, when it was placed under pontifical jurisdiction. The congregation is ruled by a superior general, who resides at Angers. Houses are located in France, Belgium, and one in London, England. The sisters are engaged in serving the sick and the poor.

Houses 23; Sisters 344; Novices 22.

8) Congregation of BENEDICTINE MISSIONARIES UNDER THE TITLE "QUEEN OF THE APOSTLES"

The congregation was formed in 1921 and remained under diocesan jurisdiction until 1946, when it received pontifical approbation. The congregation consists of three conventual priories—one each in Belgium, Portugal and Algeria, Africa—with simple dependent priories.

Conventual priories 3; Simple priories 7; Sisters 165; Lay sisters 29; Novices 13.

## B. SISTERS SUBJECT TO REGULAR PRELATE

There are only two monasteries in this classification.

1) Einsiedeln, Switzerland—All Saints Monastery, under the jurisdiction of the Abbot Ordinary of Einsiedeln. It was founded in 1526.

Sisters 53; Novices 3.

2) Ramsay, Louisiana—St. Gertrude Convent, under the jurisdiction of the abbot of St. Joseph Monastery, St. Benedict, Louisiana. It was founded in 1908.

Sisters 32; Novices 5; School 1; Pupils 45.

## C. SISTERS UNDER LOCAL ORDINARY

The monasteries are grouped according to the country in which they are located and the statistical information is given in tabular form. Since new data could not be obtained for Lithuania, the 1950 statistics were reprinted. Two sisters from Lithuania are now in Chicago hoping to make a foundation in the United States. The one monastery in Hungary was founded in 1928 but is now suppressed.

| Country | Monasteries | Dependent Houses | Sisters | Novices | Schools | Pupils | Hospitals | Patients |
|---|---|---|---|---|---|---|---|---|
| Austria | 1 | 14 | 130 | 10 | | | | |
| Belgium | 3 | 3 | 107 | 9 | 3 | 600 | | |
| Canada | 1 | | 15 | 6 | | | | |
| France | 4 | | 118 | | | | 1 | 400 |
| (Missionaries of St. Mathilde) | 3 | | 89 | 16 | | | | |
| (Sisters of Perp. Ador., Bellemagny) | 3 | 21 | 347 | 5 | | | | |
| Germany | 3 | | 89 | 14 | | | | |
| (Cong. of St. Lioba) | 5 | 36 | 323 | 30 | | | | |
| Holland | 1 | | 35 | 5 | | | | |
| Hungary | 1 | 15 | | | 5 | 600 | | |
| Italy | 4 | 5 | 246 | 26 | | | 3 | 350 |
| (Rome, Oblate Sisters) | 1 | 16 | 107 | 13 | | | | |
| Lithuania | 1 | 2 | 27 | 13 | 1 | 25 | | |
| Mexico | 1 | 16 | 120 | 19 | 4 | | | |
| Switzerland | 4 | 3 | 270 | 21 | 9 | 784 | | |
| United States | 4 | | 767 | 53 | 59 | 8,175 | 9 | 37,377 |

## CONGREGATION OF ST. SCHOLASTICA

| Location | Convent | Founded | Sisters | Novices | Schools | Pupils | Hospitals | Patients |
|---|---|---|---|---|---|---|---|---|
| Atchison, Kansas | Mount St. Scholastica | 1863 | 606 | 21 | 83 | 16,143 | | |
| Benet Lake, Wisconsin* | Holy Family | 1949 | 31 | 2 | | | | |
| Bristow, Virginia | St. Benedict | 1868 | 83 | 4 | 7 | 2,630 | | |
| Chicago, Illinois | St. Scholastica | 1861 | 185 | 4 | 16 | 6,338 | | |
| Covington, Kentucky | St. Walburga | 1859 | 233 | 9 | 25 | 6,144 | 2 | 11,073 |
| Covington, Louisiana | St. Scholastica | 1870 | 78 | 4 | 10 | 2,955 | | |
| Cullman, Alabama | Sacred Heart | 1902 | 112 | 1 | 16 | 2,906 | | |
| Elizabeth, New Jersey | St. Walburga | 1857 | 105 | 6 | 19 | 8,038 | | |
| Erie, Pennsylvania | St. Benedict | 1856 | 139 | 6 | 15 | 3,519 | 1 | 4,890 |
| Glendora, California | St. Lucy's Priory | 1952 | 62 | | 9 | | | |
| Lisle, Illinois | Sacred Heart | 1895 | 172 | 14 | 17 | 4,381 | | |
| Mexico City, Mexico | Colegio Guadalupe | 1950 | 18 | | 1 | 1,850 | | |
| Pittsburgh, Pennsylvania | Mount St. Mary | 1870 | 146 | 5 | 13 | 5,412 | | |
| Ridgely, Maryland | St. Gertrude | 1857 | 83 | 8 | 6 | 2,103 | | |
| St. Marys, Pennsylvania | St. Joseph | 1852 | 112 | | 8 | 2,623 | | |
| San Antonio, Texas | St. Scholastica | 1911 | 26 | 2 | 3 | 950 | 1 | 4,707 |
| Tinley Park, Illinois | Our Lady of Sorrows | 1953 | 20 | 2 | 2 | 600 | | |
| Tulsa, Oklahoma | St. Joseph | 1879 | 135 | 7 | 21 | 3,189 | 1 | 1,410 |

*Benet Lake is still dependent upon Tulsa, but has had its own novitiate since 1949.

## CONGREGATION OF SISTERS OF PERPETUAL ADORATION

| Location | Convent | Founded | Sisters | Novices | Oblates | Postulants |
|---|---|---|---|---|---|---|
| Clyde, Missouri | St. Scholastica | 1874 | 143 | 10 | 11 | 10 |
| Mundelein, Illinois | Blessed Virgin Mary | 1928 | 47 | | | |
| Tucson, Arizona | Christ the King | 1935 | 33 | | | |
| Kansas City, Missouri | Holy Spirit | 1943 | 34 | | | |
| San Diego, Calif. | St. Pius X | 1054 | 14 | | | |

## CONGREGATION OF ST. GERTRUDE THE GREAT

| Location | Convent | Founded | Sisters | Novices | Schools | Pupils | Hospitals | Patients |
|---|---|---|---|---|---|---|---|---|
| Arborg, Man., Canada | St. Benedict | 1912 | 91 | 5 | 6 | 535 | 4 | 3,644 |
| Cottonwood, Idaho | St. Gertrude | 1884 | 143 | 4 | 11 | 1,256 | 2 | 5,379 |
| Crookston, Minnesota | Mount St. Benedict | 1919 | 237 | 9 | 22 | 3,271 | 4 | 10,060 |
| Ferdinand, Indiana | Immaculate Conception | 1867 | 396 | 24 | 51 | 13,025 | 1 | 1,775 |
| Minot, North Dakota | Sacred Heart | 1910 | 63 | 2 | 8 | 973 | 1 | 1,324 |
| Mount Angel, Oregon | Queen of Angels | 1882 | 138 | 5 | 11 | 1,880 | | |
| Sturgis, South Dakota | St. Martin | 1889 | 92 | 1 | 4 | 903 | 3 | 11,128 |
| Waunakee, Wisconsin | St. Benedict | 1897 | 51 | 3 | | | 3 | 10,814 |
| Yankton, South Dakota | Sacred Heart | 1880 | 423 | 16 | 34 | 5,925 | 5 | 18,268 |

## CONGREGATION OF ST. BENEDICT

| Location | Convent | Founded | Sisters | Novices | Schools | Pupils | Hospitals | Patients |
|---|---|---|---|---|---|---|---|---|
| Bismarck, North Dakota | Annunciation | 1947 | 163 | 5 | 9 | 3,638 | 4 | 360 |
| Eau Claire, Wisconsin | St. Bede's Priory | 1948 | 88 | 3 | 7 | 2,195 | 1 | 1,024 |
| Nauvoo, Illinois | St. Mary's Priory | 1874 | 154 | 14 | 15 | 1,700 | | |
| Olympia, Washington | St. Placid's Priory | 1952 | 36 | | 3 | 1,062 | | |
| St. Joseph, Minnesota | St. Benedict | 1857 | 903 | 23 | 58 | 13,076 | 3 | 24,822 |
| St. Paul, Minnesota | St. Paul's Priory | 1948 | 207 | 7 | 17 | 6,164 | | |

## SISTERS UNDER LOCAL ORDINARY IN THE UNITED STATES

| Location | Convent | Founded | Sisters | Novices | Schools | Pupils | Hospitals | Patients |
|---|---|---|---|---|---|---|---|---|
| Duluth, Minnesota | St. Scholastica | 1892 | 441 | 21 | 22 | 5,135 | 4 | 37,092 |
| Fort Smith, Arkansas | Benedictine Heights | 1878 | 260 | 21 | 36 | 2,965 | 5 | 285 |
| San Antonio, Florida | Holy Name | 1889 | 47 | 5 | 1 | 75 | | |
| Bethlehem, Connecticut | Regina Laudis Monastery | 1947 | 16 | 6 | 1 (lay sister) | | 2 (Oblate sisters) | |

## PART IV

# FOUNDATIONS IN NORTH AMERICA

## STATES HAVING BENEDICTINE MOTHERHOUSES

|  | Founded |
|---|---|
| **ALABAMA** | |
| Cullman, Sacred Heart Convent | 1902 |
| **ARIZONA** | |
| Tucson, Christ the King | 1935 |
| **ARKANSAS** | |
| Fort Smith, Benedictine Heights | 1878 |
| Jonesboro, Holy Angels | 1887 |
| **CALIFORNIA** | |
| Glendora, St. Lucy's Priory | 1952 |
| San Diego, St. Pius X | 1954 |
| **COLORADO** | |
| Boulder, St. Walburga | 1934 |
| **CONNECTICUT** | |
| Bethlehem, Regina Laudis Monastery | 1947 |
| **FLORIDA** | |
| San Antonio, Holy Name | 1889 |
| **IDAHO** | |
| Cottonwood, St. Gertrude | 1884 |
| **ILLINOIS** | |
| Chicago, St. Scholastica | 1861 |
| Lisle, Sacred Heart | 1895 |
| Mundelein, Blessed Virgin Mary | 1928 |
| Nauvoo, St. Mary's Priory | 1874 |
| Tinley Park, Our Lady of Sorrows | 1953 |
| **INDIANA** | |
| Beech Grove, Our Lady of Grace | 1955 |
| Ferdinand, Immaculate Conception | 1867 |
| **KANSAS** | |
| Atchison, Mount St. Scholastica | 1863 |
| **KENTUCKY** | |
| Covington, St. Walburga | 1859 |

LOUISIANA
 Covington, St. Scholastica   1870
 Ramsay, St. Gertrude   1906

MARYLAND
 Ridgely, St. Gertrude   1857

MINNESOTA
 Crookston, Mount St. Benedict   1919
 Duluth, St. Scholastica   1892
 St. Joseph, St. Benedict   1857
 St. Paul, St. Paul's Priory   1948

MISSOURI
 Clyde, St. Scholastica   1874
 Kansas City, Holy Spirit   1943

NEBRASKA
 Norfolk, Immaculata   1923

NEW JERSEY
 Elizabeth, St. Walburga   1857

NORTH DAKOTA
 Belcourt, Queen of Peace   1955
 Bismarck, Annunciation   1947
 Minot, Sacred Heart   1910

OKLAHOMA
 Tulsa, St. Joseph   1879

OREGON
 Mount Angel, Queen of Angels   1882

PENNSYLVANIA
 Erie, St. Benedict   1856
 Latrobe, St. Emma   1931
 Pittsburgh, Mount St. Mary   1870
 St. Marys, St. Joseph   1852

SOUTH DAKOTA
 Sturgis, St. Martin   1889
 Yankton, Sacred Heart   1880

TEXAS
 San Antonio, St. Scholastica   1911

VIRGINIA
 Bristow, St. Benedict   1868

WASHINGTON
 Olympia, St. Placid's Priory   1952

WISCONSIN
 Benet Lake, Holy Family   1949
 Eau Claire, St. Bede's Priory   1948
 Waunakee, St. Benedict   1897

# THE ORDER IN WHICH EXISTING AMERICAN
## FOUNDATIONS WERE MADE

1852 St. Marys, Pennsylvania

1856 Erie, Pennsylvania

1857 Elizabeth, New Jersey

1857 Ridgely, Maryland

1857 St. Joseph, Minnesota

1859 Covington, Kentucky

1861 Chicago, Illinois

1863 Atchison, Kansas

1867 Ferdinand, Indiana

1868 Bristow, Virginia

1870 Covington, Louisiana

1870 Pittsburgh, Pennsylvania

1874 Nauvoo, Illinois

1874 Clyde, Missouri

1878 Fort Smith, Arkansas

1879 Tulsa, Oklahoma

1880 Yankton, South Dakota

1882 Mount Angel, Oregon

1884 Cottonwood, Idaho

1887 Jonesboro, Arkansas

1889 San Antonio, Florida

1889 Sturgis, South Dakota

1892 Duluth, Minnesota

1895 Lisle, Illinois

1897 Waunakee, Wisconsin

1902 Cullman, Alabama

1906 Ramsay, Louisiana

1910 Minot, North Dakota

1911 San Antonio, Texas

1912 Arborg, Manitoba, Canada

1919 Crookston, Minnesota

1923 Norfolk, Nebraska

1928 Mundelein, Illinois

1931 Latrobe, Pennsylvania

1934 Boulder, Colorado

1935 Canon City, Colorado

1935 Tucson, Arizona

1943 Kansas City, Missouri

1944 Mexico City, Mexico

1947 Bethlehem, Connecticut

1947 Bismarck, North Dakota

1948 Eau Claire, Wisconsin

1948 St. Paul, Minnesota

1949 Benet Lake, Wisconsin

1952 Olympia, Washington

1952 Glendora, California

1953 Tinley Park, Illinois

1954 San Diego, California

1955 Beech Grove, Indiana

1955 Belcourt, North Dakota

# EUROPEAN ANCESTRY OF NORTH AMERICAN FOUNDATIONS

## GERMANY

TUTZING

EICHSTÄTT

ST. MARYS,
PA.
1852

LATROBE,
PA.
1931

BOULDER,
COLO.
1934

CANON CITY,
COLO.
1935

NORFOLK, NEBR.
1923

(See following page for foundations from St. Marys, Pennsylvania)

## SWITZERLAND

MARIA RICKENBACH

SARNEN

MELCHTHAL

CLYDE, MO.
1874
(Began at Maryville, Mo.
Moved in 1876)

MUNDELEIN, ILL.
1928

TUCSON, ARIZ.
1935

KANSAS CITY, MO.
1943

SAN DIEGO, CALIF.
1954

YANKTON, S. DAK.
1880

WAUNAKEE, WISC.
1897
(Began at Sioux City, Ia.
Moved, 1953)

MT. ANGEL, ORE.
1882

JONESBORO, ARK.
1887

COTTONWOOD, IDAHO
1884
(Began at Uniontown, Wash., 1884
Moved to Cotton, Wash., 1884.
Moved to Cottonwood, 1909)

STURGIS,
S. DAK.
1889

## FRANCE

URT, BASSES-PYRENEES

JOUARRE

RAMSEY, LA.
1906

BETHLEHEM, CONN.
1944

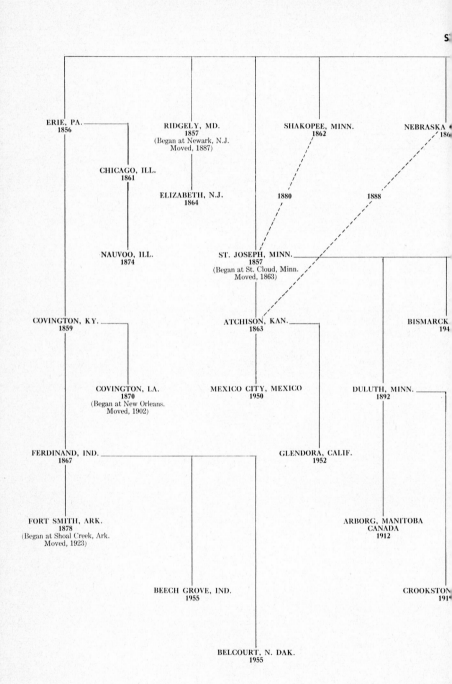

ERIE, PA.
1856

RIDGELY, MD.
1857
(Began at Newark, N.J.
Moved, 1887)

SHAKOPEE, MINN.
1862

NEBRASKA
186

CHICAGO, ILL.
1861

ELIZABETH, N.J.
1864

1880

1888

NAUVOO, ILL.
1874

ST. JOSEPH, MINN.
1857
(Began at St. Cloud, Minn.
Moved, 1863)

COVINGTON, KY.
1859

ATCHISON, KAN.
1863

BISMARCK
194

COVINGTON, LA.
1870
(Began at New Orleans.
Moved, 1902)

MEXICO CITY, MEXICO
1950

DULUTH, MINN.
1892

FERDINAND, IND.
1867

GLENDORA, CALIF.
1952

FORT SMITH, ARK.
1878
(Began at Shoal Creek, Ark.
Moved, 1923)

ARBORG, MANITOBA
CANADA
1912

BEECH GROVE, IND.
1955

CROOKSTON
191

BELCOURT, N. DAK.
1955

**A.**

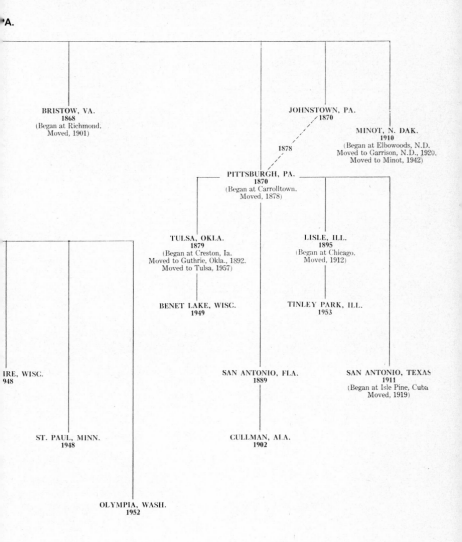

BRISTOW, VA.
**1868**
(Began at Richmond.
Moved, 1901)

JOHNSTOWN, PA.
1870

1878

MINOT, N. DAK.
**1910**
(Began at Elbowoods, N.D.
Moved to Garrison, N.D., 1920.
Moved to Minot, 1942)

PITTSBURGH, PA.
**1870**
(Began at Carrolltown.
Moved, 1878)

TULSA, OKLA.
**1879**
(Began at Creston, Ia.
Moved to Guthrie, Okla., 1892.
Moved to Tulsa, 1957)

LISLE, ILL.
**1895**
(Began at Chicago.
Moved, 1912)

BENET LAKE, WISC.
**1949**

TINLEY PARK, ILL.
**1953**

IRE, WISC.
948

SAN ANTONIO, FLA.
**1889**

SAN ANTONIO, TEXAS
**1911**
(Began at Isle Pine, Cuba
Moved, 1919)

ST. PAUL, MINN.
**1948**

CULLMAN, ALA.
**1902**

OLYMPIA, WASH.
**1952**

# LOCATIONS OF NORTH AMERICAN MOTHERHOUSES

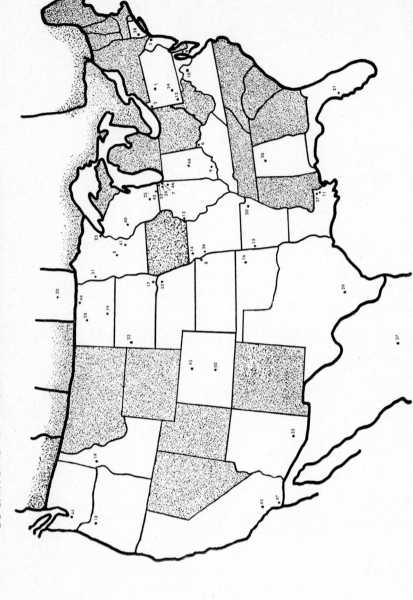

1. St. Marys, Pa.
2. Erie, Pa.
3. Elizabeth, N.J.
4. Ridgely, Maryland
5. St. Joseph, Minn.
6. Covington, Ky.
7. Chicago, Ill.
8. Atchison, Kan.
9. Ferdinand, Ind.
10. Bristow, Va.
11. Covington, La.
12. Pittsburgh, Pa.
13. Nauvoo, Ill.
14. Clyde, Mo.
15. Fort Smith, Ark.
16. Tulsa, Okla.
17. Yankton, S. D.
18. Mount Angel, Ore.
19. Cottonwood, Idaho
20. Jonesboro, Ark.
21. San Antonio, Fla.
22. Sturgis, S. D.
23. Duluth, Minn.
24. Lisle, Ill.
25. Waunakee, Wis.
26. Cullman, Ala.
27. Ramsay, La.
28. Minot, N. D.
29. San Antonio, Tex.
30. Arborg, Man., Canada
31. Crookston, Minn.
32. Norfolk, Nebr.
33. Mundelein, Ill.
34. Latrobe, Pa.
35. Tucson, Ariz.
36. Kansas City, Mo.
37. Mexico City, Mex.
38. Bethlehem, Conn.
39. Bismarck, N. D.
40. Eau Claire, Wis.
41. St. Paul, Minn.
42. Benet Lake, Wis.
43. Boulder, Colo.
44. Olympia, Wash.
45. Glendora, Calif.
46. Tinley Park, Ill.
47. San Diego, Calif.
48. Beech Grove, Ind.
49. Belcourt, N. D.
50. Canon City, Colo.

# Bibliography

References marked with an asterisk (*) appear in the original German edition either in footnotes or in the bibliography.

*Abelard, Peter. Epistola VIII (Institutio seu Regula Sanctimonialium) Migne, *Patrologia Latina* 178, col. 255 ff.

*Augustine, Saint. Epistolarum classis III, Epistola CCXI. Migne, *Patrologia Latina* 33, col. 958 ff.

Barry, Garett Francis, O.M.I. *Violation of the Cloister,* dissertation for degree of doctor of canon law. Washington, D.C.: Catholic University of America, 1943.

Baska, Sister Mary Regina, O.S.B. *The Benedictine Congregation of Saint Scholastica: Its Foundation and Development* (1852-1930). Washington, D.C.: Catholic University of America, 1935.

Bassan, Monastery of St. Jerome. *The Life of Blessed Joanna Mary Bonomo,* St. Benedict's English Daughters in Rome. Rome: St. Benedict's, 1896.

*Benedict, Saint, Abbot of Monte Cassino. *Die Oxforder Benediktinerregel,* herausgegeben von Eduard Sievers. Halle, 1887.

*Bremond, Henri. *Histoire Littéraire du Sentiment Religieux en France.* Volume 2. Paris: Bloud et Gay, 1923.

Butler, E. C. "Monasticism" in *Cambridge Medieval History,* V. 1, Ch. XVIII. Cambridge: The University Press, 1936.

*Caesarius, Saint, Bishop of Arles. *Regula Sanctarum Virginum,* ed. by Germain Morin. Bonn: Peter Hanstein, 1933. (Florilegium Patristicum, 34).

Campbell, J. A. "Virgins Consecrated to God in Rome during the First Centuries," in *American Catholic Quarterly Review,* V.25 (1900), p. 766-790.

*Catalogus Familiarum Confoederatarum O.S.B.* Rome: Sorores O.S.B. ad Priscillam, 1955.

*Canonical Legislation concerning Religious.* Westminster, Md.: Newman Press, 1948.

*Donatus, of Besancon. Regula ad Virgines. Migne, *Patrologia Latina,* 87, col. 273 ff.

Duckett, Eleanor Shipley. *The Gateway to the Middle Ages.* New York: Macmillan, 1938.

*Eckenstein, Lina. *Woman under Monasticism.* Cambridge: University Press, 1896.

Eichstätt, St. Walburg's Convent. *Spring and Harvest,* St. Walburg's Shrine, Symbol and Center of Nine Hundred Fruitful Years, translated and edited by Sister Gonzaga Engelhart, O.S.B. St. Meinrad, Indiana: The Grail, 1952.

Ellard, Gerald, S. J. "Saintly Sisters in the Shadows." *Review for Religious,* V.4 (1945) p. 155-162.

*Feussi, Iniga. *Das Institut der gottgeweihten Jungfrauen.* Freiburg, Switzerland, 1917.

*Fischer, J. L. "Entwicklungsgeschichte des Benediktinerinnenstiften Urspring" in *Studien und Mitteilungen O.S.B.,* V. 38 (1917) p. 232 ff.

Gertrude, Saint. *The Life and Revelations of Saint Gertrude.* Westminster, Md.: Newman Press, 1949.

*Heimbucher, M. J. *Die Orden und Kongregationen der katholischen Kirche.* V. 1. Paderborn: F. Schönigh, 1933.

*Hilpisch, Stephanus, *Aus deutschen Frauenklöstern.* Wien: Reinhold Verlag, 1932. (Kleine historische Monographien)

*Hilpisch, Stephanus. *Aus frühmittelalterlichen Frauenklöstern.* Düsseldorf: L. Schwann, 1926. (Religiöse Quellenschriften, fasc. 12)

*Hofmeister, Ph. "Die Verfassung der Kongregation der Benediktinerinnen von Kalvarienberg." *Studien und Mitteilungen O.S.B.,* V. 50 (1932), p. 249-277.

*Hofmeister, Ph. "Liste der Nonnenklöster der Bursfelder Kongregation." *Studien und Mitteilungen O.S.B.,* V. 53 (1935), p. 77-102.

*Jerome, Saint. Epistola CVIII Ad Eustochium Virginem. Migne, *Patrologia Latina* 22, Col. 896ff.

*Kainz, Stephan. "Nachtridentinische Reformstatuten in den deutschen Frauenklöstern der Benediktinerordens." *Studien und Mitteilungen O.S.B.*, V. 56 (1938), p. 219-274.

*Linneborn, Johannes. *Der Zustand der westfälischen Benediktinerklöster in den 50 Jahren vor ihrem Anschluss an die Bursfelder Kongregation.* Münster, Westphalia, 1898.

*Linneborn, Johannes. "Die Bursfelder Kongregation während der ersten hundert Jahre ihres Bestehens." *Deutsche Geschichtsblätter*, V. 14 (1912) p. 3-58.

*Linneborn, Johannes. "Die Reformation der westfälischen Benediktinerklöster im 15 Jahrhundert durch die Bursfelder Kongregation." *Studien und Mitteilungen O.S.B.*, V. 20 (1899) p. 1-90.

MacDonald, Sister M. Grace, O.S.B. *With Lamps Burning.* St. Joseph, Minnesota: St. Benedict's Priory Press, 1957.

Mechtild, Saint. *The Revelations of Mechtild of Magdeburg* (1210-1297) or *The Flowing Light of the Godhead,* Translated by Lucy Menzies from the manuscript in the library of the Monastery of Einsiedeln. London: Longmans, 1953.

More, Gertrude. *The Holy Practices of a Divine Lover or the Saintly Ideot's Devotions.* London: Sands & Co., 1909.

*Neues Archiv der Gesellschaft für ältere deutsche Geschichtskunde, V. 27 (1902) p. 656-669.

*Noble, L. "Historische Kommunitäten der Benediktinerinnen." *Studien und Mitteilungen, O.S.B.*, V. 54 (1936) p. 433-448.

*Pachomius, Saint. *Pachomiana Latina...* édité par Dom Amand Boon. Appendice édités par L. Th. Lefort. Louvain: Bureaux de la Revue, 1932.

*Pachomius, Saint. *Regulae monasticae,* edited by P. B. Albers. Bonn: Peter Hanstein, 1923. (Florilegium Patristicum, 16)

*Pitra, J. B., Cardinal. Analecta Sacra VIII. Monte Cassino, 1882.

*Power, Eileen. *Medieval English Nunneries,* c. 1275-1535. Cambridge: University Press, 1922.

Rudolf, Monk of Fulda. "The Life of Saint Leoba" in *Anglo-Saxon Missionaries in Germany,* translated and edited by C. H. Talbot. New York: Sheed & Ward, 1954.

Schaaf, V. T., O.F.M. *The Cloister,* a dissertation in canon law at the Catholic University of America. Cincinnati: St. Anthony Messenger Press, 1921.

Schmitz, Philibert. *Histoire de l'Ordre de Saint-Benoît,* V. 7 (Les Moniales). Belgium: Maredsous, 1956.

*Schmitz, Philibert. "Les Bénédictines" in *Dictionnaire d'Histoire et de Geographie Ecclésiastiques.* V. 7, p. 1206-1234.

Stanbrook Abbey; *In A Great Tradition.* Tribute to Dame Laurentia McLachlan, Abbess of Stanbrook Abbey. London: John Murray, 1956.

Tyburn Convent. *Tyburn Hill of Glory,* the Story of The Benedictine Adorers of the Sacred Heart and their Foundress, Mother Mary of St. Peter (Garnier). London: Burns, Oates, 1953.

# Index

# Date Due

| | | | |
|---|---|---|---|
| | | | |
| | | | |
| | | | |
| | | | |
| | | | |
| | | | |
| | | | |
| | | | |
| | | | |
| | | | |
| | | | |
| | | | |
| | | | |
| | | | |
| | | | |